CH00362009

MASSIMO LUCCHE._

Transition &
Counter Attacking
a tactical analysis

**Library of Congress
Cataloging - in - Publication Data**

by Massimo Lucchesi
  Transition and Counter Attacking

ISBN No. 1-59164-053-9
Lib. of Congress Catalog No. 2003091716
© 2003

Editing
Bryan R. Beaver

Printed by
DATA REPRODUCTIONS
Auburn, Michigan

Reedswain Publishing
612 Pughtown Road
Spring City, PA 19475
800.331.5191
www.reedswain.com
info@reedswain.com

Originally published:
April 2002
© Copyright By
www.allenatore.net
30, via Don Aldo Mei
55049 Viareggio (Lu), Italy
tel. +390584976585, fax +390584977273
e-mail: info@allenatore.net
Translation: Sinclair de Courcy Williams.

CONTENTS

Acknowledgments

The idea for this book goes back a year or two, before I finished off my work on the 3-4-1-2 and the 4-2-3-1. I must say this first of all: if I have been able to develop and elaborate on my first idea in the pages that you are about to read, it is largely thanks to **Maurizio Viscidi**. Talking with him during the last year, I have had the opportunity to evolve and broaden ideas and concepts that would otherwise have remained much more confined and cramped. Apart from being a highly skillful coach, Maurizio is also a person who clearly loves his job and who is, therefore, completely open to any discussion that will help him to expand his knowledge of concepts, aspects and details – even about questions that might seem marginal to some. As far as I am concerned, my relationship with him has been of the greatest help to me.

I am also extremely grateful to **Renzo Ulivieri**, and not only for the extraordinary and unexpected kindness that he has shown me by writing a presentation to this book. In Renzo's company, in fact, I have learnt many important things that I did not know before, and, above all, I have been so fortunate as to be able to look back in his company over situations that he has faced during his years as a coach. This has been a unique experience for me, made even more extraordinary by the sharp and minute descriptions that the coach from San Miniato was able to give me as regarding tactical problems that he has had to face during matches. It was a little like seeing the games once again as if I were in the field – or rather on the bench – and could look at the moves and countermoves taking place during a real match in Serie A, of which I remembered the highlights or the goals but only because I had seen them on TV. The Tuscan coach also taught me that:

... the really good coach does not only read the match; he can also 'feel' it.

The point is this: even though a tactical analysis is essential, it is no less important for the coach to be capable of interpreting his team's 'moments', so that he can understand when is the time to 'push it on' and when to 'hold it back', when it might be necessary to turn the locker room upside down, when it is better to keep your calm.

This is my third book, coming hard on the heels of two others that I have published in the past. If I have been able to write another book in addition to the previous two, that is largely due to the trust shown me in the past by **Fabio Frattini** and **the staff** of **Nuovo Prhomos**. The company itself, their professional know how and their quality as human beings have been a constant help to me.

Preface

I wanted to write a book and call it 'Systems Against'. I am now sorry to see that Massimo has got there first.

Such a great variety of systems are used in the Italian championship that every single match is full of 'Transition and Counter Attacking'. In my long career I have used every playing system that Massimo deals with in the book, and looking at these pages, I have been able to read about things that I have often put into practice on the field. The book explains things in a simple way – and it will help readers to survey the tactical development of a match more clearly while they are sitting on the grandstand or in front of a TV.

I recommend it to coaches, but also to those fans (and there are many of them) who enjoy watching a match from the point of view of the coach.

Renzo Ulivieri.
*(Coach of Bologna,
Parma, Torino)*

Introduction

In this book I will be trying to highlight what I consider the most important things that a coach must keep in mind when preparing the team's defensive strategy.

In the pages that are to follow I have given full treatment to theoretical concepts, but I have also tried to imagine what would be the most effective defense strategies to use when one playing system meets another.

Needless to say, the examples that I give here cannot take into account the various strengths and weaknesses of the players that make up my hypothetical team or that of our opponents.

My advice, therefore, is to read the book in an intelligent way, attempting to draw out what you think might be right or useful in relation to the conditions in which you are working.

Whatever move or countermove the coach makes will prove useful only in so far as it manages either to set off the abilities and attitudes of the players on the team or to limit those of the opponents.

Massimo Lucchesi

Chapter 1

Important tactical principles for counteracting your opponents' system

Regaining ball possession.

The main aim of the defense phase is, of course, to regain possession of the ball without a goal being scored against you.

A defending team can take back possession in various ways, through
the direct or indirect intervention of one or more players, goalkeeper included. Of course, it is never the best thing to recover ball control as the result the goalkeeper's intervention, and so here is a list of
the other ways of doing so:

- A move made by a defending player in order to get the ball
  out of his adversary's possession;
- A move made by a defender managing to control a vacant
  ball;
- The intervention of the referee, awarding a free kick to the
  defending team following on a foul committed against them.

In the table below, we have completed this classification, filling it
out with other subdivisions.

A CLASSIFICATION OF THE WAYS IN WHICH A TEAM INVOLVED IN THE DEFENSE PHASE CAN REGAIN BALL POSSESSION	
Moves made by the defender the moment that the ball arrives, or when it is still under the adversary's control	• Anticipation • Contrast
Moves made by a defender intercepting a loose ball	• Intercepting a pass • Intercepting a loose ball after a contrast, an imprecise reception or a bounce
Rules infraction by the opponent	• Ball goes out of touch • Offsides • Foul committed by the attacker

Team organization.

It will be easier to regain possession of the ball if all the teammates take part in the play, observing their directives and the collective principles that they have worked out in advance.

Looking at the ways of taking back possession as set out above, we can see at once that over and above the ability of the single player, it is very important that you have good collective organization. Here are a couple of examples. In order to retrieve ball possession due to the **irregular position** of one or more of your opponents, the whole team – and the defense section in particular – must be good at moving up together so that the adversaries will be left offside. The team's ability at keeping a short distance between the various sections on the one hand, and doubling up systematically on the player in possession on the other, will favor recovery of the ball by **contrasting, interception of loose balls** or **bad passing**.

Good offensive pressing makes it difficult for the opponents to build up play, and forces them to utilize long or badly judged passes or even to put the ball out of play by mistake. In cases like these, the defenders will have less trouble regaining possession as a result of **anticipation, interception of the ball** or **fouls committed by the adversaries**.

We must always keep in mind that besides making it easier to regain possession, good defensive organization will be fundamental in cases where the team is having to face critical or tactically complicated situations.

The 'compact' team.

Reducing the space and playing time – both for the opponent in possession and for his nearby supporting players – is an important factor in gaining ball control.

We have already had a look at the ways in which we can recover possession. The first figure (FIG. 1) shows how much easier it will be to take back possession when the various sections of the team are playing close together. The fact is that, besides reducing the adversaries' space and playing time, the 'compact' team makes it much easier for the players to:

1)   Cover each other when they must 'risk' **going out in anticipation**: the closer together the players are the smaller the distance they have to cover when one has to move up and the others are forced to stand in for him.

2)   **Double up** more often and with greater effectiveness: a 'compact' team favors speed, and makes it easier to double up, due to the simple fact that the players involved in the defense phase are covering shorter distances in moving back and forth.

3)   **Control** those areas of the field when it is more often possible to get possession of loose balls: if the players are close together it will be easier for them to cover the opponents' passes and take up position in the spaces near the ball.

4)   **Cover** the ball, i.e., putting a player near the opponent in possession, ready to intervene if he should manage to get past his direct defender.

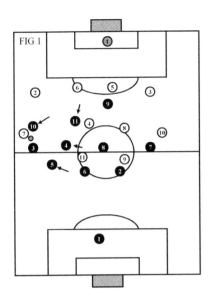

The opponent with the ball.

The tactical situation is this: any player on the opposing team is in possession and wants to develop play. Theoretically speaking, he can:

- play the ball by bringing it forward, gaining depth of field;
- play the ball without gaining depth of field, but trying to keep possession and if possible to improve his own and his team's subsequent prospects of creating play.

Techniques used for developing play might be:

- a forward pass;
- a dump shot or backward pass;
- running with the ball (keeping ball possession while gaining depth);
- dribbling (keeping ball possession and moving forward after having got round one or more opposing players);
- defending and keeping possession of the ball (without gaining depth)

A CLASSIFICATION OF THE WAYS IN WHICH THE PLAYER IN POSSESSION OF THE BALL CAN DEVELOP PLAY IN THE ATTACKING PHASE	
PASSING	• Forward (assist) • Backward (dump)
KEEPING POSSESSION	• Dribbling • Attacking with the ball • Defending the ball

The aims of a team in the defense phase.

When a team is trying to regain possession these are its aims:

- aggressive marking of the player in possession in order to limit his playing space and tempo (even by doubling up the marking);

- anticipatory marking of opponents near the ball so as to give them less opportunity to play it (closing up the lines into which they can pass the ball, and placing players in the adversary's 'shadow' areas;

- using 'ball coverage' so that it is easier to intervene if the player in possession manages to dribble past a player;

- controlling the parts of the field near the ball, where it is possible to get back possession by intercepting loose balls or making the most of any technical errors that might come about (mistaken passes, bad ball control, fumbled attempts at dribbling etc.).

If the players involved in the defense phase can implement these aims with continuity, it will be difficult for the opponents in possession of the ball to carry out the plays that they are trying to achieve (as classified in the table above). At the same time the adversaries will have trouble developing the principle sub phases (building up, finishing touches and shooting) that make up the attacking phase.

Shifting position in the defense line.

Shifting is the principle tactical ploy of the defense phase. If shifting is carried out with the **right timing** the players can then double up with effectiveness, put 'coverage on the ball', control the areas near the ball and carry out pressing by 'covered anticipation of play'.

TACTICAL AIMS THAT CAN BE ACHIEVED BY MEANS OF SHIFTING	
Carried out at the right moment, SHIFTING leads to:	• Doubling up • Ball coverage • Control of the area near the ball • Covered anticipation of play

'Shifting' (or switching) is the move of one player (or of an entire section of the team or a vertical chain) which changes position, closing in on the area where the ball is in play, or placing itself in a zone that is tactically more important.

In the following example (FIG. 2) we see a 'shift' carried out by the player in coverage. He is closing in on the player in possession who has just beaten his direct opponent. The two other players in the defense line shift over and the side mid-fielder on the weak side of

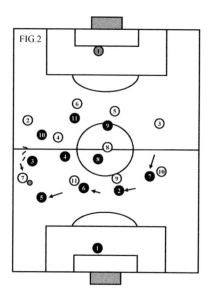

FIG.2

the field (the side without the ball) switches down to take up position in a part of the field that is strategically more useful at this point.

Depending on whether one or more players are involved in the move, we can speak about three different types of shifts:

• Horizontal shifts
• Vertical shifts
• Combined shifts

Horizontal shifts concern only the section of the team in question, aiming to bring the players nearer to the ball (FIG. 3).

Vertical shifts are carried out by a chain of players. They have the same aspirations as horizontal shifts, and can move players up or back. Forward shifts are useful when you need in-depth pressing or you want to 'force' a situation that is unfavorable. Backward shifts are generally for pressing in the lower part of the field. (FIG. 4)

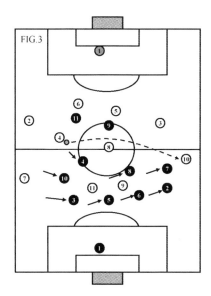

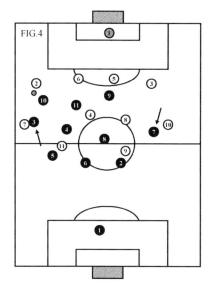

Combined shifts take place when the team wishes to effect the two preceding types of shifts at the same time. It is possible (and very often even advantageous) that the players should reduce their opponent's playing space by using combined horizontal and vertical shifts. In the example (FIG. 5) we can see how the defense line moves to the right (horizontal shift), while, at the same time, the side mid fielder nearest to the player in possession doubles up on him (vertical shift) and the side mid fielder on the opposite line moves back (vertical shift)

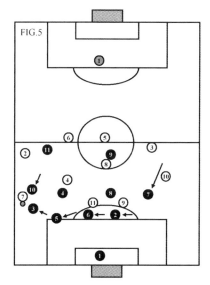

into the position left free by the side back who has now moved into the middle following his section's play.

The technical and tactical ability of the individual as an essential basis upon which to improve the effectiveness of the defense phase.

In order to shift in an effective way and with the right timing, the players must be able to 'lengthen' the marking on the weak side of the field, using what is called 'T-shaped' marking.
This is only a small and fairly ordinary example to illustrate how the individual abilities of the single players are indispensable to the efficiency with which the team carries out its strategic aims during the defense phase.

Confrontation between two systems of play: strategic choices to be made by the coach.

Two things are necessary when counteracting the opponent's system of play: individual skills of the players and an efficient team strategy. Of course, besides finding out all we can about the system used by their opponents, the team will be able effectively to contrast their adversaries only if they also know as much as possible about the distinguishing features of the players they are to meet. If we are acquainted with the strengths and weaknesses of our opponents, we can then work out the moves that will enable us to limit their effectiveness of play without distorting our usual tactical set up. Let's say, for example, that our team normally uses the 4-3-3 system, and our adversaries on this occasion are applying the same set up. We are aware that their left side back, knowing that the center mid fielder can cover for him, very often accompanies attacking play and will be a thorn in our side. A good counter move at this point, so as to make sure that the side striker does not have to tire himself out in what for him is the unaccustomed work of coverage, could be to centralize the wing, putting him in cover on the attacking mid fielder, and to tell the right center mid fielder to counteract the assaults of the side back. We will then need a consequent horizontal shift of the whole middle section (the central mid fielder moves up to oppose his direct adversary, while the left side mid fielder will move down as a screen in front of the defense section).

Having had a good look at our opponent's system and the way in which the members of the team put that system into effect and by comparing these with our own scheme of play and with the players we have at our disposal, we will now be able to decide the best shifts and / or tactical moves for our team to make.

IN ORDER TO DECIDE ON THE BEST DEFENSE STRATEGY TO USE THE COACH WILL HAVE TO:	
THE WORK OF THE COACH	• Have the opponents' system as clear in his mind as possible; • Know as much as possible about the plays (support, assistance) carried out by the interpreters of the system; • Establish the part of the field where numerical superiority is to be created, and from which his team will put most pressure on their adversaries; • Define the shifts that will be most efficacious to this end; • Fix on novel solutions or alternative tactical situations.

In the examples that are to follow we will not be in a position, obviously, to talk about the players' strengths and weaknesses, and we will only be having a look at some possible shifts that can be made in order to create numerical superiority near the ball.

Counteracting the opponent's system.

As we have already seen in the first part of the book, a compact team will find it easier to set up the conditions (doubling up, covering the ball, covered anticipation, control of the zone) which lead to numerical superiority near the ball so as to be able to regain possession.

When the team is playing against a particular system the coach will have to:

•   Carry out a tactical analysis so that he can identify the situations of numerical inferiority and superiority (in each section of the team and in each part of the playing field) that might come into being as a result of the two opposing systems of play.

•   Decide in exactly what part of the playing field it might be useful to create numerical superiority and therefore start to press. As a consequence of this decision he will have to accept the existence of numerical equality in defense in certain tactical situations – either that or rethink his conclusions.

•   Underline the best ways of shifting so as to be in a position to double up, cover, anticipate while maintaining coverage or controlling certain areas.

Depending on his own philosophy of play or on the technical and tactical strengths and weaknesses of his team, the coach will be able to:

- Activate a defensive strategy based principally on his team's ability to shift correctly so that they can create numerical superiority in the area of the ball.
- Activate a defensive strategy that foresees an initial situation of numerical superiority in the defense zone, with consequent tactical counter moves in other parts of the field.

In the first of these two cases, the coach favors a defense strategy based on pressing and on the ability of his players to cut down on the opponent's playing space and time. In the second, the coach wants to have a situation of numerical superiority in the defense zone, and to carry out a 'stand by' strategy, based on the control of the parts of the field near his own penalty area, and on his players' adaptation to the opponent's system.

Apart from considerations concerning single interpretations of the defense phase, I think we can divide teams into two general categories:

- Teams that utilize an aggressive defense;
- Teams that utilize 'stand by' defense.

Aggressive teams are those that begin the very moment they lose possession to carry out shifts and go into incessant pressing so that they can drive their opponents into a predetermined area of the field.
'Stand by' teams, on the other hand, apply a strategy that makes

much less use of forward shifting. Moving backwards, they look for numerical superiority in the ball zone, using pressure (in particular, doubling up and ball coverage) only when the attacking team arrives at a certain distance from the goal.

We must also underline the fact that, depending on the result and the psycho-physical condition of the players, the team should always be able to change its attitude as the match proceeds.

Aggressive Defense

An aggressive team will always try to put pressure on the opponents as soon as they get possession. The advantages of this type of playing system derive mainly from the following factors:

1)   the player gaining possession may not yet be in complete control of the ball;

2)   if the player has regained possession in or around his own penalty area, his tension and the negative consequences involved in losing it again will often induce him to make bad plays or long passes;

3)   the moment a player gains possession he probably does not yet have the necessary points of reference on the field to know the exact location of the players that can help him clear the ball.

A perfect application of offensive (or ultra offensive) pressing will doubtless bring many advantages with it; but we must admit that there are drawbacks as well. In particular, if we are to carry out aggressive defense:

1) the players must be able to move quickly and with synchronism; and that will only be possible as a result of hard and continuous work during training sessions;

2) the team must be in excellent psycho-physical condition;

3) the team must understand that by attacking in depth they will at times be running risks in defense (situations of numerical equality, offside, etc.).

Here, then, is an example of how to shift in order to carry out aggressive pressing when both teams are using the 4-4-2 system.

Situation: opponents' center back in possession.

The nearby striker attacks a defender in possession forcing him to play onto the sidelines or to opt for a long pass (the player to whom the ball has been directed will have difficulty controlling it first of all; and as well as that it will favor the defender's anticipatory move).

Situation: opponents' side back in possession.

If the center back manages to pass the ball to the side back, then our side mid-fielder must go into pressing on him while our side back moves up, shortening the team and covering the opponent's side mid fielder. At the same time, our center mid fielder nearest to the ball blocks the

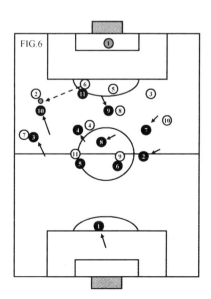

FIG.6

passing line towards the center (closing in on the opponent's center mid-fielder); the most distant striker moves backwards to cover the center mid-fielder who is furthest from the ball; and our free center mid-fielder goes back to shield the defense and to control an important area of the field should the opponents be forced (or choose) to go for a long pass. In the central defense zone we have a situation of numerical parity (our two central defenders are covering the two strikers) with the back on the weak side of the field (i.e., the opposite side to the one where the ball is being played) running in towards the center to take away space in case the strikers should manage to free themselves of marking and to intervene if there is any sudden change in the tactical situation.

'Stand by' defense.

Lying in wait for your opponents to make a mistake, (or, should we say, the application of defensive pressing so as to induce the adversaries to lose possession), will mean, of course, that you must be particularly good at doubling up, at controlling the area around the ball and at 'covering the ball' so that the defender involved in contrasting the player in possession can be as aggressive as possible. In the following examples we will be illustrating useful shifts carried out by a team using the 4-4-2 whose opponents are adopting the same system.

Situation: opponents' side mid-fielder in possession.

If he is being marked by the side back (as in Fig. 7) then, as we see, the side mid-fielder should move back to double up; the center mid-fielder blocks the passing line towards the inside of the field, acting as a defensive shield; the defense line positions itself in such a way that the left center back can cover the ball. If, on the other hand, it is our side mid-fielder who is contrasting the opponents' mid-fielder – our side back will mark the striker aggressively in his zone of play, and the central mid-fielder will shield the defense, at the same time giving coverage to the ball.

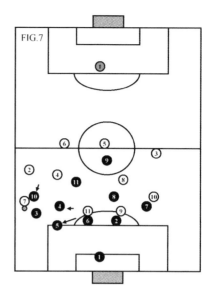

FIG.7

Situation: striker in possession.

If the striker receives the ball centrally, back to the goal, the nearest mid-fielder moves back to double up and the defense line uses the other center back and the nearest side back to give ball coverage.

If the striker manages to turn (or receives the ball) facing the goal, then his marker must intervene, supported at all times by the players covering the ball.

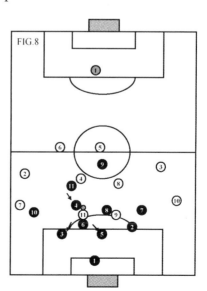

FIG.8

Chapter 2

Counteracting with the 4-4-2 system

Counteracting with the 4-4-2

We will begin our overview of the possible solutions to adopt when facing teams using various different playing systems by imagining that both our team and the opposition are lined up with the 4-4-2.

The tactical situation.

The first thing to point out is that our defense line will be playing in numerical superiority against the opposing strikers (4 > 2); in mid-field the two teams are employing four players each, giving a situation of numerical equality; and the adversary's four man defense line confronts our two strikers. Dividing the field into vertical lines (Fig. 9) we see that the two opposing systems generate a natural situation of numerical equality. Along the sidelines both our side backs and our side mid fielders have to counteract the adversary's players in the same positions. In the central zone our two backs will be taking care of the two opposing strikers (just as our own two strikers will be contrasted by the same number of opposing center backs), while the two pairs of center mid fielders will be fighting it out among themselves. This is the 'natural' situation created by the system with which the two teams have been positioned on the field.

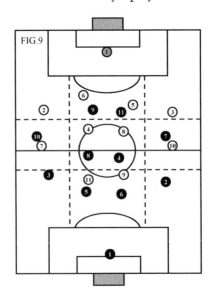

FIG.9

We can now have a look at what possible defensive shifts might be carried out in order to create more favorable tactical situations.

<u>Shifts to create numerical superiority.</u>

Some examples of shifts to be carried out in order to create numerical superiority around the ball:

Fig. 10 shows how the defending team has managed to create a situation of numerical superiority both near the ball (by doubling up) and in the more enlarged area around (a 3 > 2 situation in the center of the mid field and in the center of the defense).

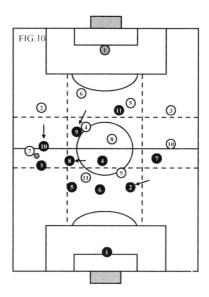

The next two illustrations give further examples of how to create numerical superiority near the ball and in the more important zones around.

By centralizing the left side mid fielder while at the same time bringing back the striker you can create a favorable 4 against 2 situation in the area of the ball.

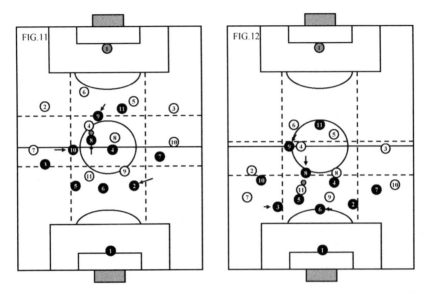

Again, in Fig. 12 we see how to build up numerical superiority in the ball zone by using combined shifts.

The next figure shows how the team can shift so as to storm the opponent with offensive pressing. The team succeeds in its aim: the close up marking of supporting players near the ball and the creation of numerical superiority in the central mid field and defense zones.

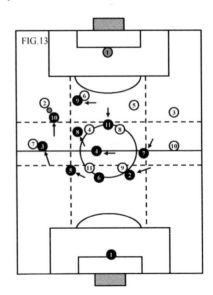

<u>Focal points.</u>

Quite apart from any questions of technical ability and athletic quality, if you want to prevail from a strictly tactical point of view against a team lined up with a playing system identical to your own, you must get the better of them in timing and in the precision of your shifts. It is particularly important when facing a 4-4-2 to succeed in transforming the many situations of numerical equality into conditions of numerical advantage for the team by the incessant use of doubling up and effective shifting in the area of the ball. Should the coach realize that his team is not able to handle the opponent's play by making the necessary shifts, or if the team keeps finding itself 2 against 2 in the central area of the defense, it might be a good idea to change the situation, turning the original 4-4-2 into a 3-5-2 or a 5-4-1. In such a case, we will be forced, of course, to use a 'stand by' defense system, but we will have the advantages of: 1) finding ourselves in numerical superiority in defense; 2) being able to deal out specific tasks to specific players; and 3) not having to depend too much on the quality of our shifts.

THE 4-4-2 AGAINST THE 4-3-3.

Proceeding with our analysis of the various solutions that can be used when we a facing a specific system, we will now consider how our team should react when facing the 4-3-3.

<u>The tactical situation.</u>

We can see at once that our defense section will be playing in numerical superiority over the opponent's strikers (4 > 3); in the

mid-field our four players will
face the three of our adversary's;
while a four-man defense line will
be controlling our two strikers.
Dividing the field into lines (Fig.
14) so that we can analyze the
tactical situation, we see that our
two center backs are in numerical
superiority as regards the opponent's central striker, with our
side backs occupied in a man to
man duel with the opposing

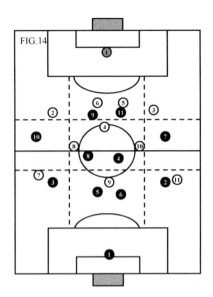

FIG.14

wings. In the mid field we are in numerical inferiority in the central
zone (2 < 3), while in attack the opponent's center backs will be
controlling our two strikers, and their side backs will be ready to
shift down in coverage over our side mid fielders.

Shifts to create numerical superiority.

Here are some examples of how to create numerical superiority in
the area of the ball:

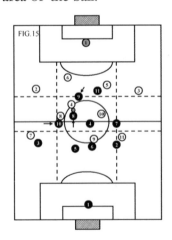

FIG.15

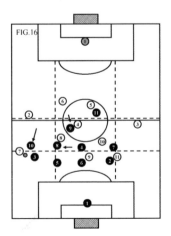

FIG.16

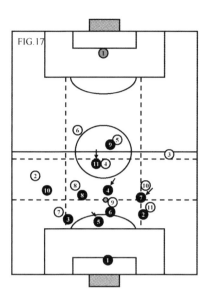

Figure 18 shows a shift carried out by the team in order to attack the opponents with aggressive pressing. We must mark the support-

ing players around the ball as tightly as we can, and we have created numerical superiority in the central zones of the mid field and the defense.

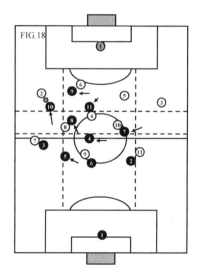

<u>Focal points.</u>

When facing the 4-4-3 our mid field must be compact so as not to suffer a 2 < 3 situation in the central zones – as well as to create numerical superiority there (4 > 3). For the same reason, it is impor-

25

tant that the center mid fielder nearest to the ball should always be able to shift with speed and precision onto the opposing central player to make sure that the side chain of the 4-4-3 (consisting of the side back – the central mid fielder – the wing) is never in numerical superiority with respect to our two side players. The mid fielders must be able to move backwards and double up on the wings and the central strikers. In any situation where the team seems to be in difficulty in the mid field, having trouble limiting the adversary's numerical superiority, a useful solution might be to place the mid fielders in a rhombus formation (being very careful about shifting when the side defenders of the 4-4-3 insert themselves into play), or to change the original 4-4-2 into a 4-5-1, which may be more appropriate to the opponent's lineup.

THE 4-4-2 AGAINST THE 3-5-2.

Let us now have a look at how the 4-4-2 faces the 3-5-2.

The tactical situation.

The first thing we can see is that our defense section is in numerical superiority on the field against the attacking strikers (4 > 2). At the same time, however, the opponents can try to exploit the 2 against 2 situation that is created in the center. In the mid field our four players are in numerical inferiority both as a section in itself (4 < 5) and in the central zone (2 < 3), while in attack our two

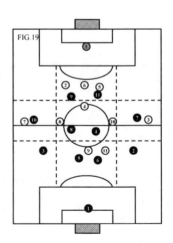

strikers are being covered by the three central defenders who will be in numerical superiority. On the sides the 4-4-2 has numerical superiority over the 3-5-2, with the side backs and side mid fielders who can play against a single opponent on each of the adversary's sidelines.

Shifts to create numerical superiority.

Figures 20, 21 and 22 give some examples of how to employ combined shifts in order to create numerical superiority around the ball.

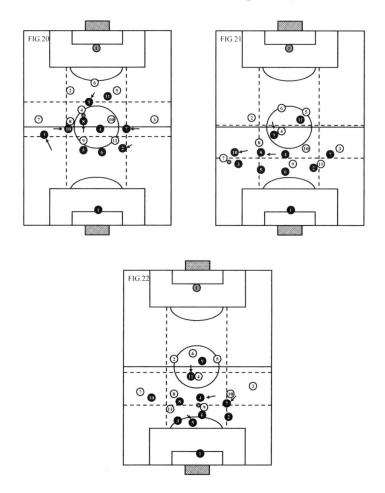

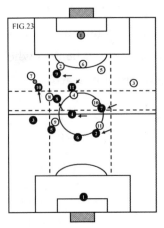

Figure 23 shows a forward shift, carried out by the team in order to storm the opponents. Here the team is able to mark the opponent's supporting players around the ball as closely as possible, and has created numerical superiority in the central parts of the mid field and the defense.

Focal points.

The side defenders' shifts are the really important element when facing the 3-5-2. These must be able both to centralize their play so as to guarantee numerical superiority (3 > 2) against the opposing strikers, and to move forward to make up for the numerical inferiority in the center. In order to create superiority in the mid field, side backs must go into depth of course, but it is vital that the second striker should move back as well so that he can cover the opponent's attacking mid fielder. If our team lined up as a 4-4-2 is not particularly quick and adept at this type of shifting it is possible to modify the position of the side backs (centralizing one and moving the other up) so that the original 4-4-2 becomes a 3-5-2 like the adversary's. A solution of this type gives us a tactical situation that we can manage more easily with numerical superiority (3 > 2) in the defense area and well defined individual clashes in the middle of the field.

THE 4-4-2 AGAINST THE 3-4-3.

We will continue our consideration of the various solutions to be adopted when facing particular systems by imagining that our team is now playing against opponents who are using the 3-4-3.

The tactical situation.

First of all, we can see that our defense section will be playing in numerical superiority against the opposing strikers (4 > 3); in the mid field our four players will face the same number on the other team; and our two strikers are playing against the three defending backs. Basically, both teams are playing with numerical superiority in defense and the same number of mid fielders will be facing each other in the center

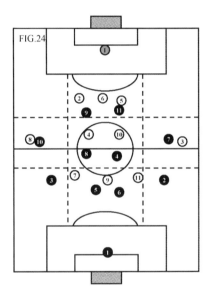

of the field. Taking a look at the tactical situation divided in vertical lines, we must first establish whether the three-man attack of the 3-4-3 is going to play 'tight' or not. With a tight three-man attack (as in the examples we are about to consider) our team will have numerical superiority over the side players and inferiority in the central part of the defense (Fig. 24).

<u>Shifts to create numerical superiority.</u>

In the following illustrations we will be having a look at some examples of how to create numerical superiority around the ball.
Figure 25 shows how the side players should tighten in so as to create numerical superiority in the central area. Figure 26 indicates a
useful shifting move to make when the opposing side mid fielder is
in possession.

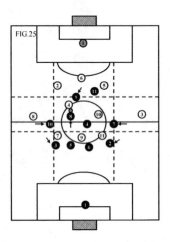
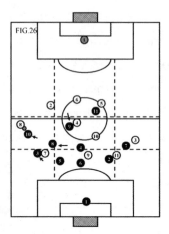

In figure 27, we can see the mid fielders
vertical backward shift permitting them
to go in coverage of an active area of
play.

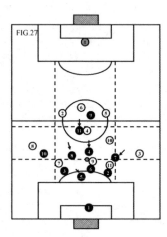

30

Figure 28 shows the team's forward shift into depth to bring immediate pressure on the player in possession. On the strong side (where the ball is being played) we can see the aggressive marking brought to bear by our players over their direct adversaries. We should highlight the movement of the striker N° 9, who, by moving sideways onto the opposing back, forces him to play the ball in the

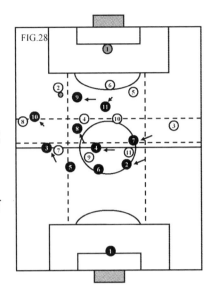

desired direction. In the mid field we can clearly see how the N° 8 puts the opposing N° 4 under pressure making it difficult for him to support the player in possession, and how the right side mid fielder places himself to shield the defense.

Focal points.

Both teams have numerical superiority in defense and four mid fielders at the center. It is vital, therefore, that the mid fielders should double up on the opposing strikers. The mid fielders and the backs should play near to each other in horizontal lines so that the opposing mid fielders and strikers will have reduced space and time for their plays. If we want to set up good offensive pressing the team must play close together both in width and depth, with a striker moving back on the opposing attacking mid fielder so that the center mid fielders can create superiority around the ball. When a 4-4-2 is playing against a 3-4-3 the tactical situation is fairly clear; in order to have superiority in the mid field, it might be a good idea,

31

however, to change the original 4-4-2 into a 4-4-1-1 (with an attacking mid fielder who, in the defense phase, is 'working' on his opposing number, thus assisting our mid fielders' shifts to double up on the opposing strikers). Another change you might make is to choose a 3-5-2 lineup (permitting us to place five men on the center line in support of the three man defense unit who are counteracting the three strikers playing tight).

THE 4-4-2 AGAINST THE 3-4-1-2.

We will conclude our overview of playable solutions with the 4-4-2 by having a look at what happens when we have to face an opponent playing with the 3-4-1-2.

The tactical situation.

The biggest single problem to handle when facing the 3-4-1-2 is how to control the attacking mid fielder, who, moving between the two lines of the mid field and defense, can create numerical superiority in both areas of the field, as we can see from Figure 29. To compensate for this handicap there is, however, the advantage to be drawn from the fact that we can count on two side players on each flank, who will be in numerical superiority against the adversary's single man in that area.

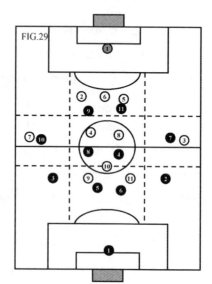

FIG.29

Shifts to create numerical superiority.

In the following figures we will be having a look at some examples
of shifts that can create numerical superiority in the ball zone.
When the ball is in the central part of the field (Fig. 30), our team's
tactical situation is fairly negative for the simple reason that we are
facing a situation of structural
numerical inferiority. The diagram
shows how the side players
should shift horizontally so as to
turn that situation round. In
order to limit the attacking mid
fielder's playing space and time,
we can counteract him, as we will
see later, by moving one of the
two center backs forward, or by
moving one of the internal mid
fielders back. This, of course, will
alter the tasks and the placement
of the side players. If you decide that the center back should move
up to put pressure on the attacking mid fielder, then the two side
backs must move in and play tight and close to the remaining center
back so as to contain the two opposing strikers. If, on the other
hand, the center mid fielder moves down in coverage on the attacking mid fielder, then the side mid fielders must centralize their position, with the side backs ready to absorb any cuts that the rival mid
fielders might try to make.

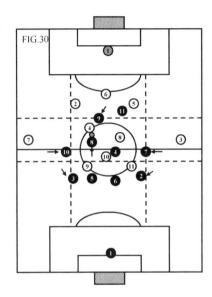

FIG.30

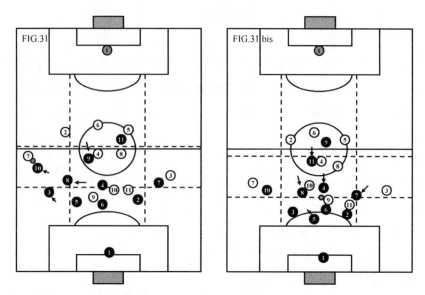

The following figure (Fig. 32) shows the shifts to use when you want to press the opposing team in depth, in cases where their side back is in possession. The striker N° 9 goes against him to put him under pressure, forcing him to play the ball to the side where our pair N° 10 and N° 3 will be in numerical superiority.

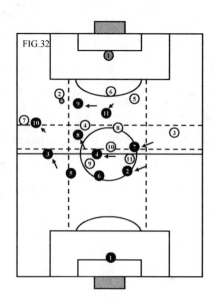

<u>Focal points.</u>

We have already seen that the greatest problem for the 4-4-2 is the control of the attacking mid fielder. In my opinion, there are, as we have already seen, two different solutions to the problem of how to limit his playing space and time:

- We can decide to put him into the care of the two mid fielders, whose appropriate shifting moves will restrict his ability to free himself of marking and to play the ball.
- We can get the center back to move up and put him under pressure.

Both these solutions will need suitable coverage on the part of team mates. In the first case in particular, a striker must move back into the area of the attacking mid fielder so that we do not feel numerical inferiority in the center; either that or the side players should move towards the center. In the second case (the central back moving into depth) the defending section most remain compact horizontally because a side back will have to take on the striker who has been left free when the center back moves up.

We could also imagine the following 'structural revolution' with the 'creation' of an asymmetrical 4-4-2 as the result of these tactical modifications:

1   decentralizing a striker out onto the sidelines (or moving him back between the lines);
2   moving up the two side players on the opposite flank;
3   bringing down the two side players on the flank where the striker will be playing 'wide'.

These moves will force the opponent's defense section to transfer a player onto the flank and to bring back a side mid fielder into the defense phase, thus modifying the set up of these two sections. The coach using a 3-4-1-2 system could also decide to play in numerical equality in defense, with all the risks that would involve (cf. Fig. 33), above all considering that the backs will be unable to guarantee adequate coverage on account of the wide spaces that separate one player from another.

In the defense phase one of the two lateral chains of the 4-4-2 can be brought backwards so as to guarantee the defense section's numerical superiority or equality (depending on the shifts we are adopting to contrast the opponent's attacking mid fielder) over the adversary's attacking players.

We should point out that our decision to put the striker wide or to bring him back between the lines will depend on the particular attitude of the player first of all, but also on the tactical stance that we wish to take up in the defense phase.

In fact, if our striker is 'floating' between the lines and moving down during the defense phase to counteract an opposing attacking mid fielder who is playing far back, then we can assign to whichever of our center mid fielders has the greater defensive sense more work in coverage and control of the adversary's finishing touch player (or even inverting that job with the team mate of that section, should the player in question take up position in the opposite part of the field). However, the center mid fielder is not the only player who should be trying to counteract the opponent's finishing touch player: our numerical superiority in the defense zone (3 against 2) will permit us to bring up a back whenever the tactical situation should require it. The fact that we have numerical superiority is also important because it will allow us to close in on the inserting plays of the striker with a certain confidence.

The tactical decision to put a striker wide on the sidelines will result in him no longer being able to counteract the attacking mid fielder. That in its turn will mean that in the mid field the opposite finishing touch player has to be contrasted by the nearest center mid fielder to his zone of play, and that our central defender must intervene in any attacking plays.

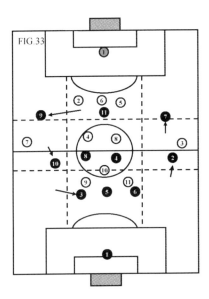

Another solution that we could use when facing the 3-4-1-2 is to place five men on the mid field line, changing the original 4-4-2 into a 3-5-2 or a 4-5-1. If we adopt the 3-5-2 system that will make the tactical situation clear (numerical superiority in the defense zone and well defined clashes in the central zone); should we go for the 4-5-1, that will mean accepting a 2 against 2 situation in the central part of the defense (the central player of the five-man mid field goes back in coverage on the attacking mid fielder) in order to have numerical superiority when counterattacking along the sidelines.

Chapter 3

Counteracting with the 4-3-3 system

Counteracting with the 4-4-3.

THE 4-3-3 AGAINST THE 4-4-2.

The first example that we are to consider is the 4-3-3 system counteracting the 4-4-2.

The tactical situation.

As we can see (Fig. 34) the situation on the field is 4 against 2 at the level of our defense section. In mid field our three players will have to deal with four opposing numbers, while our three strikers are trying to get past a four man defense system. Looking carefully at the situation divided into vertical lines we can see that our three central mid fielders can create a favorable situation in that zone. On the other hand, we will have to be very careful about any 2 against 2 situation that might come about when our two center backs would be taking on the pair of opposing strikers. The side backs will need to be good players with a great sense of timing and tactical intelligence in order to shift at the right moment and set up a situation of numerical superiority (3 against 2) to the advantage of the defense. Another problem that we will have to resolve is the control of the opponent's side mid fielders. There are various ways of closing in on them. In the defense phase we could bring down a side strik-

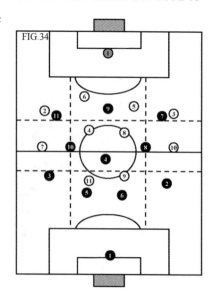

FIG.34

er or move up a side back or even slip our nearest center mid fielder over to the side in question. These are all satisfactory solutions, and only our experience of what to expect from our adversaries compared with the particular abilities of our own players will tell us which is the right option for us to use. We can also define a certain number of shifts to carry out in order to create numerical superiority in or around the area of the ball when the opponent's side player is in possession. In Fig. 35 we can see how our center mid fielder moves sideways to double up on the player in possession, who is being contrasted at the same time by our side back coming out into depth on him. At the same time, our wing is coming back in order to close the lines and make it more difficult for the player in possession to dump the ball on the central mid fielder. We could, however, do the very opposite – and have our wing move back to double up, sending our center mid fielder in coverage on his opposite number to make sure the ball will not be dumped on him. A third possible solution would involve the participation of the central striker in the defense phase; he would move back in coverage on the opposing mid fielder, with our central mid fielder remaining as a shield in the area around the ball.

Shifting moves to create numerical superiority.

In this first example of a possible shift – which we have already looked at in detail above – the opponent's center mid fielder is in possession.

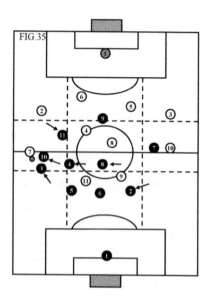

If an opposing central mid fielder is in possession we can bring in our nearest central mid fielder at the same time keeping both numerical superiority in the ball zone and a player (our center mid fielder) in front of the pair of central defenders to shield them. The most difficult problem to resolve is how to contain the opposing side mid fielders. Seeing as our mid field is in numerical inferiority against our opponent's cor-

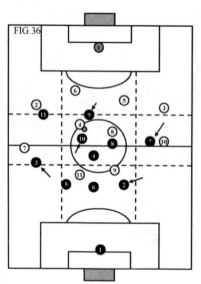

responding four man section, we are going to have to organize the right shifts in order to counterbalance the situation. We can see in Fig. 36 how the opponent's side mid fielders are to be marked by bringing up a defender on the strong side of the field and calling the wing down on the weak side. There are other solutions that we could use as well, like bringing both wings back or getting the two side backs to move up at the same time. Two considerations will help us make the best decision: the match situation and our study of the strengths and weaknesses of the players themselves.

Figure 37 shows the plays to be made by a team using the 4-3-3 when the ball has been given to one of the opponent's strikers. We can see the center mid fielder moving back (so as to double up) and the right side back moving in – both plays that will create numerical superiority in the ball zone. The central mid fielder N° 8 goes out onto the side to compensate for N° 2's movement towards the center and to save N° 7 from having to move too far back.

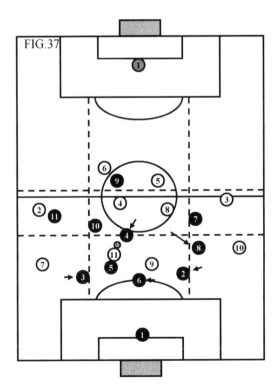

In the last illustration (Fig. 38) we see the team's forward shifts in order to attack the opponents with aggressive pressing. We are succeeding in our aim to mark the opponent's supporting players as closely as possible near the ball and to create numerical superiority in the central zones of the mid field and the defense.

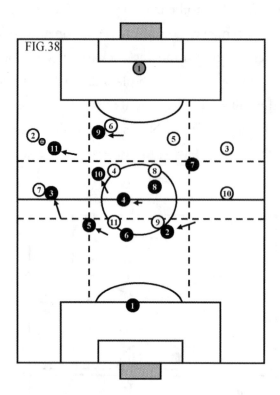

Focal points.

If our team's shifts cannot contain the opponent's play it might be a good idea to intervene as far as the playing system is concerned in order to improve things and make our counteraction more effective. The two things that we will have to be very careful about when facing a 4-4-2 are the effectiveness of our shifts to make sure that the mid field does not suffer numerical inferiority against the oppo-

44

nents, and the team's ability to manage the two opposing strikers both individually and collectively. In cases where the team can't seem to contain the two opposing strikers or whenever the side mid fielders of the 4-4-2 have too much playing space, we can change the original 4-3-3 into a 4-5-1 by bringing back the wings, or we could even transform it into a 3-4-3, bringing up a side back or putting a center mid fielder more onto the sidelines. The first of these two solutions guarantees numerical superiority in the center of the field (5 against 4), while the second option favors a type of counteraction that will be less connected with the team's effectiveness in shifting, in that each player will be up against one adversary in his own area of competence with the defense playing in numerical superiority against the two opposing strikers.

THE 4-3-3 AGAINST THE 4-3-3.

Moving on with our analysis of how to face different playing systems, let us now have a look at the situation when we have to play against a team using our own system: the 4-3-3.

The tactical situation.

The tactical situation on the field is relatively clear: the defense section is playing in numerical superiority over the rival strikers (4 > 2) and there is numerical equality in the mid field (3 against 3). As both teams will be operating a low attacking line, one of the problems we will come up against is how to keep the team as compact as we can. Another problem to resolve is connected with the fact that the wing must not come too far back when he is following the attacking runs of the opposing side defender.

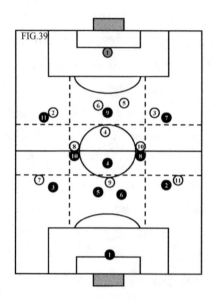

Shifting moves to create numerical superiority.

The first example shows the movements the team must make when the opposing center mid fielder is in possession. The central striker moves back forcing the adversary to control the ball while under pressure, which could allow our center mid fielder to advance and double up on him.

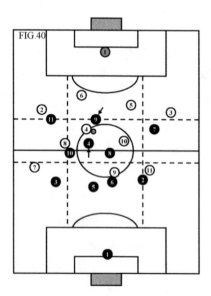

The second example shows the shifts made so that the wing does not need to move too far back as he follows the opponent's side defender as he goes forward into attack.

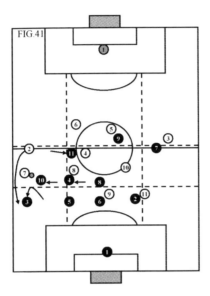

The mid field section's horizontal shift will allow us to counteract this move with effectiveness. They shift over to the wing who is in possession, with our N° 10 leaving his usual adversary so that he will be able to follow the movements of his rival counterpart. Our left wing will be able to participate in the defense phase without having to move too far back; he will close up on the opposing center mid fielder who does not usually go very much into attack but normally works as a supporting player.

In Fig. 42 we see an example of how our team should behave when the opposing center striker is in possession. Here, the center mid fielder moves back to double up.

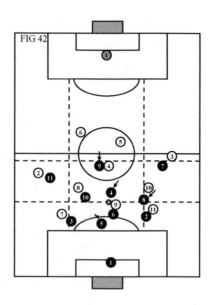

The last example shows shifting moves so as to carry out in-depth pressing. The center striker is placed half way between the left center defender and the center mid fielder, ready to intervene (moving promptly as the pass is being effected) should the side back decide to dump the ball on either of those two players. The wing should

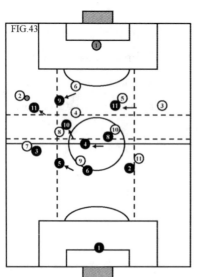

put the player in possession under pressure by moving out of the center in order to force him to play the ball along the sidelines, so cutting the opponent's N° 4 out of the action.

Focal points.

As we have already said, the tactical situation on the field is relatively clear, and will not require special shifting moves, in that each player has his own opposing point of reference. It is important, therefore, that the team can move together and with good tempo. One of the characteristics of the 4-3-3 is the great variety of attacking combinations that the trident can create. Our defenders must be able to regulate the strikers' range of movements, and must be good at neutralizing the dangerous cuts of the wings, which – the ball flying diagonally in between the side and central backs – can often penetrate right into the heart of our defense and create terrible difficulties for us. Should our team have problems controlling the opposing three-man striking group there are basically two things we can do:

•   we can personalize the marking of the rival strikers with one player separating himself and acting as a sweeper;

•   we can bring back the wings, changing the 4-3-3 into a 4-5-1. This solution gives us numerical superiority in the center of the field and will help us to double up on our opponent's side strikers. The idea is to cut down on our rival mid fielders' space and playing time, making it difficult for them to manage the ball or filter dangerous balls through to the strikers.

A third possible solution if our team has lost control of the match might be to bring back a wing and to widen out a center mid fielder, changing the 4-3-3 into a 4-4-2. That will give us numerical superiority in the center of the field, especially if our two strikers are playing vertically, with the second ready to slip back and cover the opposing center mid fielder during the defense phase.

THE 4-4-3 AGAINST THE 3-5-2.

The tactical situation.

After having divided up the field as usual, we will notice that our four-man defense is facing the opponent's two central strikers; in mid field our situation is unfavorable (3 against 5); and our opponent's three-man defense section will be containing our three strong attack. Taking a closer look at the 'vertical' situation, we see that the opposing strikers can exploit the 2 against 2 situation

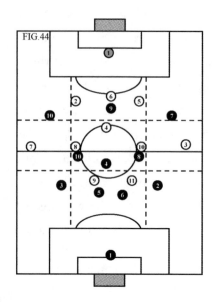

that is created centrally. In the mid field the central zone is 3 against 3, but our biggest problems will come about as the result of the freedom the opposing side players will have if our team is unable to make the right shifting moves. In attack, our three strikers may find good playing space and be able to get through the three-man defense, especially if the adversaries are unable to shift correctly in order to control the sidelines. The 4-3-3 and the 3-5-2 are systems that do not go very well together on the playing field, and so, in my opinion, the weaker of the two teams will have no option but to adapt itself. More particularly, the coach of the team using the 4-3-3 will have to choose one of these three solutions in order to close in on the opposing side mid fielder in possession:

- bringing back the wing;
- bringing up a side back;
- decentralizing the entire mid field.

Each of these solutions has its advantages and its disadvantages and we will be able to make the right decision only on the basis of what we know about our players' specific characteristics or when we find ourselves in a particular situation on the field.

<u>Shifting moves to create numerical superiority.</u>

In the following figures we will be having a look at some examples of shifts that will help create numerical superiority around the ball. As we have already suggested, the team will be required to do different types of shifts depending on how the players are to be placed on the field – at what depth they are to go into pressing, for example, or, exactly how far back the wings have been told to play. In the examples that we are giving the wings will not actively participate in the defense phase but will remain in depth so that they can counterattack through the spaces left by the opposing three-man defense.

The last figure in the series shows our players shifting in order to attack the opponents with offensive pressing. Our center mid fielder moves out on the opponent's side back in possession; our wing moves forward to double up and our center forward moves back a yard or two putting himself in the vicinity of the opposing center mid fielder, ready to go into attack between the spaces if we happen to regain possession.

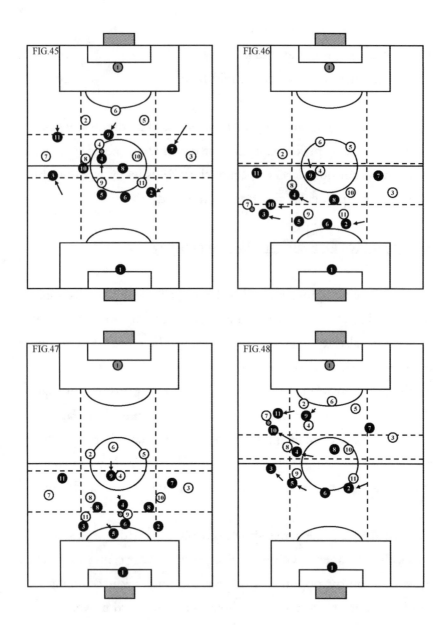

52

Focal points.

The most important things to keep in mind when the 4-3-3 is facing a team that uses the 3-5-2 are the following:

- the team's ability to make sure that the opposing strikers are not playing in numerical equality (2 against 2) in the face of our two central defenders;
- the team's ability to shift along the sides in order to take away space and playing time from the side players
- our team's ability, when in possession, to attack the opponent's three-man defense by bringing the wings into play.

If the coach sees that his team is giving way under the opponent's play and is not able to shift or counterattack, he should then consider modifying his tactical set up.

The original 4-3-3 can be turned into a 4-5-1 by bringing the wings back nearer the opposing side mid fielders. This solution will simplify the work and the shifts of the mid fielders and makes it easier to double up on the sidelines.

If the defense section is having trouble stopping the rival strikers, a possible solution would be to copy our opponent's system, changing our original 4-3-3 into a 3-5-2 by moving a wing back and bringing the side defender on the same flank more towards the center. He will place himself near the center defenders, so creating a three-man section able to play in numerical superiority against the two opposing strikers. On the opposite side of the field, instead of bringing the players back, we will ask the side back to advance (bringing him into line with the mid fielders), with the wing moving towards the center to give the center forward a hand.

THE 4-3-3 AGAINST THE 3-4-3.

We will now have a look at how the 4-3-3 will face an opponent using the 3-4-3 system.

The tactical situation.

Looking at the set up section by section shows us that our defense will have numerical superiority (4 backs against 3 strikers). That situation is turned upside down in the mid field to our disadvantage (3 against 4). Our three-man attack will have to get through a defense section made up of the same number of players. Dividing the field into vertical strips we can see at once that our defense could find themselves (if the side backs do not shift with the right sense of timing) in numerical inferiority in the center. In mid field, our opponents might find space along the side-lines thus creating numerical superiority for themselves. It should also be said, however, that our three-man group of mid fielders could create problems for the opposing pair. Lastly, by playing 'wide' our three strikers could

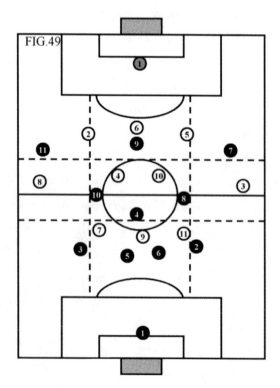

FIG.49

find good spaces (in particular along the sidelines) and put the opponent's defense in serious danger.

Shifting moves to create numerical superiority.

In the following figures we will be having a look at some examples of how to create numerical superiority in the area around the ball. In figure 50 we see the central striker moving back to double up on the opposing center mid fielder already under pressure from our own center mid fielder. In this way, our team has created numerical superiority in the area around the ball. Our left side mid fielder (N° 10) will be covering the mid fielder on the strong side of the field, and our right side back is ready to move up on the opponent (N° 3) playing on the weak side. We should point out that if our N° 10 had gone in pressure on the player in possession, then our left side back would have had to move up on the opponent's N° 8 and our whole defense section would have

had to slide towards the left, with the right center mid fielder (the N° 8) ready to move wide in coverage of the opposing side mid fielder (the N° 3) on the weak side of the field.

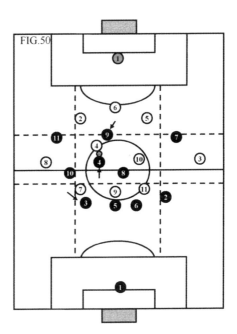

FIG.50

Fig. 51 shows how the side back can move out on the opposing side mid fielder. By doubling up on the same player the wing creates numerical superiority, while our left side mid fielder goes in on the opposing mid fielder N° 4 so that the player in possession can no longer dump the ball on him. The fact that the ball is 'covered' makes it possible for our N° 10 to move up.

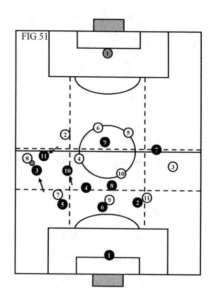

Our defense section is drawn up man to man, shielded by the center mid fielders. We are not, in my opinion, running too great a risk playing 3 against 3 in defense because our opponent's compact three-man attack will give us enough shifting time should we need it.

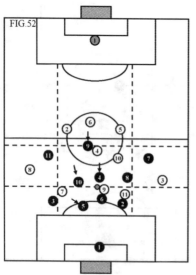

Fig. 52 shows shifts carried out in order to create numerical superiority over the three man attack when the ball is in the defense zone.

Fig. 53 is an example of ultra-offensive pressing by our team. N° 9 and 11 go into pressure on the ball and the whole team slips over onto the strong side.

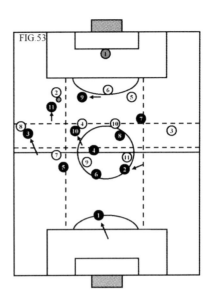

Focal points.

The following is what we are aiming at when facing a 3-4-3:

- to make sure, using the most suitable shifting moves, that the opposing three-man attack never finds itself in numerical superiority over our two central defenders:
- to be able to shift up on the opposing side mid fielders, taking playing space time away from them;
- to see to it that our highly offensive three-man attack can exploit the spaces that the opposing three-man defense section will, of course, concede.

We must define our attitude to pressing and to where we should begin to apply it. If the opposing defense section is attacked with the right tempo by our three strikers, they will probably find it difficult to organize their movements and keep the ball circulating. On the other hand our numerical inferiority in mid field may create some problems for our pressing in that section, especially if our shifting moves are not carried out with perfect synchronism. The coach will have to decide if is better to apply offensive or ultra-offensive pressing (with the three strikers putting on the pressure and the side back on the strong side moving up to stop the opposing side mid fielder); or whether it might be more appropriate to deploy a 'stand by' strategy, with the mid fielders doing most of the pressing. This second option will involve a gradual backward movement of the team, with the wings slipping down and integrating themselves with the mid field section in order to create a positive situation there (5 > 4) making it easier to regain possession in that part of the field. Here are a couple of alternative solutions that may improve the situation if our team is in difficulty and cannot seem to stand up very well to the adversaries. We have already seen that bringing the wings back into line with the mid fielders will help us in that section and make it easier to regain possession. But the 4-3-3 can turn itself into a 4-4-2 as well, by bringing only one wing back, putting the mid fielder on the opposite side to play out wide and bringing the other side striker in towards the center so that he will be able to give the central striker a hand. These moves will give more balance to the situation in the center of the field, thus simplifying the side backs' shifting moves and making sure that they will have to worry much less about moving up to go and contrast the rival side mid fielder.

THE 4-3-3 AGAINST THE 3-4-1-2.

We will conclude our overview of the defense solutions that can be put into practice using the 4-3-3, having a look at the tactical situation when our opponent's line-up is the 3-4-1-2.

The tactical situation.

Examining the situation zone by zone, we can see that, though our defense section has numerical superiority (4 > 2), it might have problems in the center where it is 2 against 2. In the central part of the mid field there is numerical equality (3 against 3), but at the same time the opposing side players will have space. Our three-man attack is facing a defense section consisting of the same number, and stopping our strikers will be the most difficult problem our opponents will have to resolve. As far as our team is concerned, playing against the 3-4-1-2 will mean three things: trying to limit the playing space and tempo of the opposing side mid fielders first of all; secondly, making sure that the two opposing strikers do not find space in the center of our defense; and lastly, succeeding in exploiting the spaces a three-man defense will concede to our three strikers.

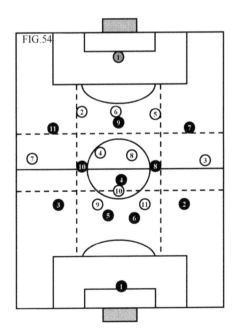

FIG.54

Shifts to create numerical superiority.

In the following figures we will look at some examples of how to create numerical superiority in the area around the ball.

In the first example, Fig. 55, we see how our 4-3-3 brings back the center striker to create numerical superiority around the ball, with the left side back moving into depth and the wing on the weak side coming down. The decision to bring the wing on the weak side back is a consequence of the fact that the right side back will have to move towards the center so that the two center backs are not playing in numerical inferiority against the two opposing strikers and the attacking mid fielder who is moving in.

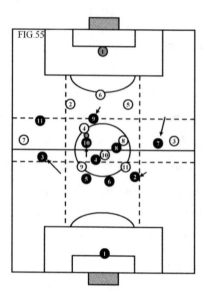

Fig. 56, on the other hand, shows out team's shifts made so that we can double up on the opposing side mid fielder in possession. The left center mid fielder moves towards the sidelines to give a hand to the side back N° 3, who is contrasting the player in pos-

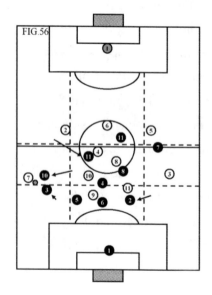

session, while the wing N° 11 (the third part of the lateral chain) goes backwards to cover the opposing N° 4, a player in support.

Fig. 57 shows the right side mid fielder (the player nearest to the ball) doubling up on the player in possession. The center mid fielder (N° 4) is keeping an eye on the attacking mid fielder, and the right wing (who must follow the movements of the vertical chain) and the left side back are limiting the two opposing side mid fielders' playing space.

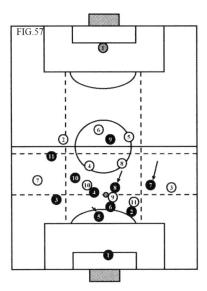

In the last example (Fig. 58), we see the movements of the team during the phase of in-depth pressing. The defense is tight on account of the shifting movements of the mid fielders (with the center mid fielder leaving go of the attacking mid fielder in order to close in on his supporting player N° 4).

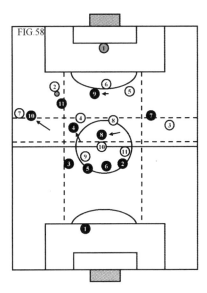

Focal points.

On the field, the 4-3-3 and the 3-4-1-2 are systems that create tactical situations which neither team will be able to sustain for long. The fact is that the side players of the 3-4-1-2 will have a lot of space to play in, and that may oblige their opponents, lined up as a 4-3-3, to adapt their play. In the same way, the three-man defense of the 3-4-1-2 will find it difficult to face the wide attacking front of the 4-3-3, and this might force the coach to modify his system. In order to confront the 3-4-1-2 with success, confining the opponent's side mid fielders and the 2 against 2 situation at the heart of our defense, it is vital that we keep the team compact so as to assist the shifting moves that we have already had a look at. Another important question to keep in mind is the effectiveness of our three-man attacking line. If our three strikers are managing to put the rival's defense under fairly constant pressure, we may decide to let them have a few yards on us. On the contrary, if our opponent's backs are getting the better of the play it might be a good idea to change our original setup. We could bring back our wings, transforming the original 4-3-3 into a 4-5-1. This solution will take something away from our potential in the attacking phase, but it will give us more balance in the mid field, limiting the space and playing time that our opponents had before.

Chapter 4

Counteracting with the 3-5-2 system

Counteracting with the 3-5-2

THE 3-5-2 AGAINST THE 4-4-2.

We will begin our analysis of tactical moves to be used with the 3-5-2 system by imagining that we have to meet a team lined up as a 4-4-2.

The tactical situation.

In the most important part of the field (the mid field) the 3-5-2 has numerical superiority as a section in itself (5 > 2) and also in the central area (3 > 2). By moving up and breaking into play, however, the opposing side backs could create problems for our single players on the lines, creating a situation of numerical inferiority which would be to our disadvantage. This will be one of the problems that we will have to resolve when facing the 4-4-2, avoiding at all times such a situation of numerical inferiority on the sidelines by carrying out the right shifting moves. In defense our three-

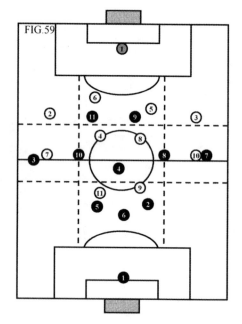

FIG. 59

man section is having to do with two opposing strikers and will therefore be able to count on a good situation of numerical superiority (3 > 2). Lastly, in attack our two strikers are facing two central backs supported by side defenders ready to close all space with diagonal plays. All this can be clearly seen in figure 59.

<u>Shifting moves to create numerical superiority.</u>

As we have already said, when facing the 4-4-2 it will be necessary to check the situation of numerical inferiority that comes about when the opposing side back moves up to cooperate with the side mid fielder. What generally happens in such cases with teams using the 3-5-2 is that our side mid fielder covers the opposing side mid fielder and our nearest center mid fielder goes wide to take on the opposing side back who is in possession. At this point we balance the situation of numerical inferiority by having our other center mid fielder move onto the side. It is important that some other variations should follow on these so that side back in possession does not find his team's center mid fielder (who is supporting play) too free of any kind of marking. In other words, our team must be trying to do two things at the same time: firstly, they are re balancing the numerical situation along the sidelines, and secondly, they want to make sure that the opposing center mid fielder does not receive the ball too easily. For these two reasons:

- our center mid fielder must move up. As shown in Fig. 60, he is going into depth at the same time as the central midfielder who plays alongside him, i.e., when the second goes out wide onto the sidelines, the first moves in onto the center mid fielder.

- our two strikers must organize themselves as best they can: one goes in coverage on the nearby center defender to make it difficult for the player in possession to dump on him; the other moves back onto the opposing center mid fielder who is supporting play – both plays shown in Fig. 61.

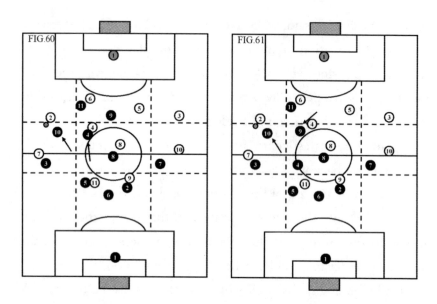

If the coach decides to shift upwards by having the center mid fielder move into depth, it is important that he should point out how the shield in front of the defense then disappears. It is a good idea, therefore, that the players marking the two opposing strikers should shorten the distance between them and their direct opponents, if possible, placing themselves in position beforehand. In any case, the third back, (sometimes called the 'free' defender) will be able to cover the defense section adequately should the strikers make short or in depth passes.

Another possible shift, in order not to find ourselves in numerical inferiority along the sidelines, is to move our side player into depth (in coverage on the opposing player in possession), followed by our defender's immediate shift out on the adversary's side mid fielder (fig. 62). This is certainly a more aggressive shift than the last and it may be useful when you need to 'force' a situation. We should note that as a result of this type of shift we will have a 2 against 2 situation in defense. The remaining center mid fielder's work as a shield will then become important with the other having moved up to cover the opposing player in support (the nearby center mid fielder).

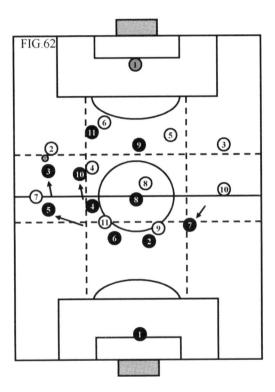

As we have already seen, the 3-5-2 system has a natural numerical superiority in the central part of the defense and the mid field (3 > 2). It is a good system to play with if you want to create continuous doubling up and to put your opponents under pressure by positioning players in such a way as to anticipate them in these parts of the field. The following figures will give some examples.

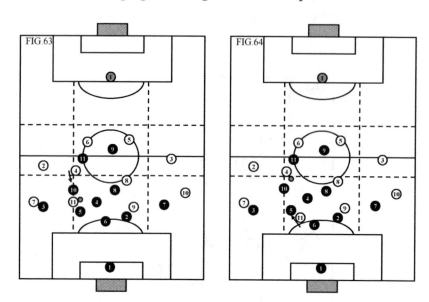

Focal points.

As we have already made clear in the preceding pages, our team will be in a much better position if they manage to stop their opponents on the sidelines (where most of the play will systematically tend to develop). On the contrary, should our shifting moves prove unable to contain our opponent's play, we must modify our original system. If the coach wants to play with a three-man defense in any case, then the only other system that in itself can block our numerical inferiority along the sidelines is the 5-4-1. Playing like that the tasks and the plays of our three-man defense will remain practically the

68

same, while along the sidelines what was originally our only external player will now be able to dedicate himself to the control of the rival side mid fielder, with our side mid fielder ready to absorb the opposing side back's forward incursions.

THE 3-5-2 AGAINST THE 4-3-3.

We will continue with our study of the tactical moves to be adopted by the 3-5-2 system having a look at how to face a team using the 4-3-3.

<u>The tactical situation.</u>

Looking at the tactical situation that appears naturally on the field as shown in Fig.. 65, the first thing that you will notice is the situation of numerical equality (3 against 3) that we will have to put up with in defense. It is not impossible for a three-man defense successfully to counteract three opposing strikers playing wide, though of course this situation is by no means ideal. In order to contain the adversary's attacks our defense section will have to be tactically proficient and individually capable as well as being mentally prepared to overcome certain difficulties. In particular, the side backs must be able to close in on the wings the moment the

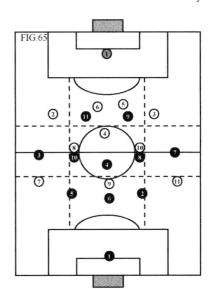

FIG.65

ball is being passed to them to make sure there are no open spaces in the central areas. When they arrive near the player in possession, the side backs must manage to contain the opposing side strikers' attacking charges, their dribbling and their in-depth plays. Taking a glance at the situation in the other parts of the field, we can see that our mid field section is in marked numerical superiority over our opponents (5 > 3). In the attacking zone, our two strikers are working against our opponent's four-man defense section. Here, the two central defenders will be kept busy (in a situation of numerical equality 2 against 2) if our system manages to play in advance by bringing our side mid fielders into depth and forcing the opposing side backs to play wide.

Shifting moves to create numerical superiority.

In my opinion the 3-5-2 and the 4-3-3 are two systems that do not combine well on the playing field, and so the management of the match may not be too easy. In order to play well in the defense

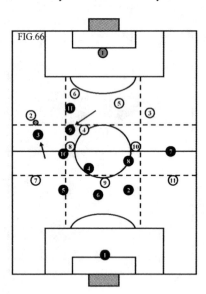

FIG.66

phase, we will have to make a clear-cut decision about the team's attitude and the depth at which our two side mid fielders should be playing. If we feel that we can accept a 3 against 3 situation in defense and can therefore play in an aggressive way, we will tell our two side mid fielders to play in depth, attacking the opposing backs as soon as the ball goes in their direction. If we decide to play the match in that way, our central mid fielder's and our two strikers' tactical intelligence will become important. The first will place himself as a shield in front of the defense, and the two strikers will have to place themselves in a vertical line so that the opponent's supporting players (the nearby central defender and the center mid fielder) cannot receive the ball too easily.

If, on the other hand, we decide to play the match in a more pru-dent way, then we will ask our two side mid fielders to act as the fourth and fifth defender, which will make the team's whole attitude more cautious. In this case our pressing will be defensive, and will principally involve the mid fielders moving back to double up – the central mid fielder will go to help the center back, doubling up on the striker they are covering, while the two side mid fielders will assist the two side defenders, doubling up on the wings.

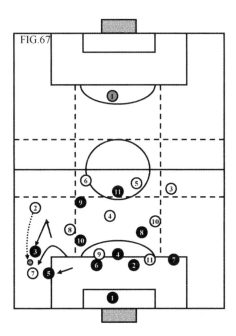

<u>Focal points.</u>

If we choose to be more aggressive, we will have to keep a very close eye on exactly how effective our defenders are in containing the three opposing strikers – both as a group and as individual players, . If they are having difficulty it might be a good idea to modify the team's strategy (using defensive pressing), or to change the system. To counteract a 4-3-3 without having to do too much shifting you can copy their placement on the field using a 4-4-1-1.

On the contrary, if we have decided for the more prudent attitude, it will be important to make sure that the pressing in the mid field is really effective and to verify that we are counterattacking well. Here again, if the team is being forced into an attitude that seems too passive because the players are not shifting correctly, then we should adapt ourselves to the situation modifying our playing system.

THE 3-5-2 AGAINST THE 3-5-2.

We will now have a look at a situation where we are facing a team playing with the same system as our own.

<u>The tactical situation.</u>

A tactical analysis of the situation on the field shows us that:

- the two teams have numerical superiority in defense. The three central defenders are controlling a two-man attack;
- the two teams are playing in numerical equality in the midfield. In particular, in the central zone we have a natural situation of 3 against 3, while on the sides the players of each team will be 1 to 1 against their direct opponents.

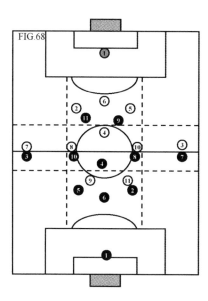

FIG.68

Shifting moves to create numerical superiority.

When we find ourselves playing against a team using our own tactical system, the winning element will be the quality and the effectiveness of our shifts. Only if we can turn the many 1 to 1 duels that there will be in the mid field to our favor, will we be able to seriously consider winning the match. If our shifts are not perfect the team with the better players will come out on top – or the team that prevails in the 1 to 1 combat in the vital areas of the mid field. Fig. 69 gives an example of various shifting movements made to create favorable situations of numerical superiority in the cen-

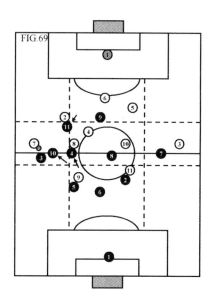

FIG.69

tral and side zones. Our side mid fielder goes in pressing on the opposing side mid fielder in possession. We can even create a positive situation of 2 against 1, if our nearby left inside mid fielder slips over to double up, with our center mid fielder going in coverage on the opposing center mid fielder and the two strikers taking up a vertical position to close off a dumping pass. There will be no shield in front of the defense, but that can be made up for by the aggressive attitude of the men who are marking and who have their backs covered by the sweeper. If the ball arrives to the strikers we can create numerical superiority by bringing back the nearest mid fielder.

Fig. 70 illustrates a 'forced' shift, resulting from the aggressive attitude of the pressing. Our side mid fielder moves up on the opposing defender in possession. As he is doing this, our inside mid fielder goes wide in coverage on the opposing side mid fielder while one of our strikers closes off a supporting player – the center mid fielder N° 4 – and the other blocks off the possible dumping pass on the center back N° 6.

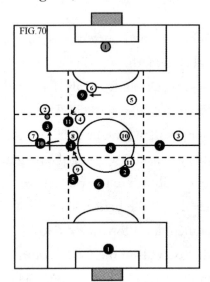

FIG. 70

<u>Focal points.</u>

As we have already said, when two teams using the same system of play are lined up on the field, it will be the more technically gifted of the two that will probably come out on top. We can overturn the situation, making the technical gap insignificant, only if the our shifting moves are effective enough to compress our opponent's playing time and space. If our team is not able sufficiently to contain the opponent's play, it is very important either to change the system in use or give new life to the individual duels by substituting players. What the coach actually decides to do in order to resolve the problem will depend on the specific difficulty the team is having. As an example, if we are fighting a losing battle on the sidelines, we could try to resolve the situation in the following ways:

- substituting a player who is having difficulty with one whose particular strengths make him better able to limit his direct adversary.
- changing the 3-5-2 into a 4-4-2 so as to have two players on each side who can cooperate in containing a dangerous opponent.

Clearly, it is the coach who will have to make up his mind which is the best decision, on the basis of the problem in itself and of the contingent situation.

THE 3-5-2 AGAINST THE 3-4-3.

Going on with our survey of the moves and countermoves to be made by a team playing the 3-5-2 system, we will now have a look at how they will face a 3-4-3.

The tactical situation.

Both teams are using a three-man defense. Yet, while our backs are playing in numerical equality against three strikers, our two strikers are in inferiority against our opponent's defense (2 < 3). Looking at the face off in mid field we can see that there will be a situation of numerical equality on the sidelines (1 against 1) and a situation of numerical superiority favorable to us in the central zone (3 > 2). The situation is clearly represented in the figure below.

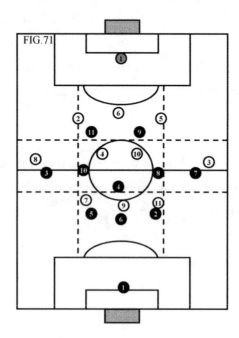

<u>Shifting moves to create numerical superiority.</u>

As we have already mentioned during our survey of the 4-3-3 it is important to decide whether or not to accept the situation of numerical equality in the defense zone. We should point out, however, that the three strikers of the 4-3-3 are not normally placed in the same way as those of the 3-4-3. Initially, the three strikers of the 4-3-3 occupy the whole offensive front with the wings ready to converge towards the center so as to attack in depth or receive the ball between the lines and then filter it through or run forwards in possession. The three-man attack of the 3-4-3 on the other hand, usually plays in quite a compact formation so as to exploit combinations and allow the side mid fielders to come into depth with or without the ball. This strong difference in organization will have a clear cut effect on the way the strikers (in particular those on the wings) will move in order to get free of marking; and that in turn will, of course, rebound on the defenders' tactical behavior. A three-man defense that consents to play in numerical equality against the compact group of three opposing strikers will certainly find it easier to make good diagonal passes.

In cases where we cannot accept a situation of numerical equality in defense, the coach will have to tell the players what type of shifts to play so as to bring an extra player into the defense line. In my view, the possible shifts to be made in order to create a $4 > 3$ in the defense zone are the following:

- move back a side mid fielder (presumably the one playing on the weak side);
- bring back our center mid fielder in order to create a $2 > 1$ in the center.

Clearly, we will have to establish the type and the depth of our defensive pressing on the basis of whether or not to include a fourth element in the three-man defense.

In the following figures we can see two examples where the opposing right mid fielder is in possession and our team carries out two different types of shifts. Fig. 72 shows a team that feels at

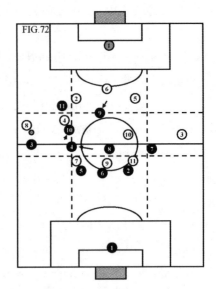

ease with the 3 against 3 in the defense zone. The mid field section slips over towards the ball zone to take playing time and space away from the opposition.

Fig. 73, on the other hand, shows how to integrate the right side mid fielder into the defense line. In this case, the team is playing a watchful game, making sure that our two side backs do not have the time to cover too many yards (inverting their tactical roles) if the opposition start passing the ball around.

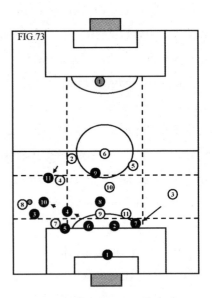

Fig. 74 is an illustration of our team's forward shifting in order to produce aggressive play. Naturally, the choice of whether or not to play in numerical equality in defense has no importance in this case, because at this point the team is moving forward, shifting its center of balance into depth. Looking carefully at the figure, it is important to notice how the inside mid fielder moves

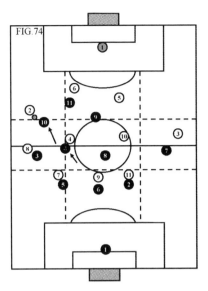

up on the opponent's back in possession, our center mid fielder then slipping into depth so that he can take away playing space and make it difficult for the opposing center mid fielder to receive the ball. In other situations, we have seen our side mid fielder shifting into depth, but, tactically speaking, that is not a good idea in this case, because the 3-5-2 system has a single player on the sidelines. For that reason, and because of the situation of numerical equality in defense, we must not bring up a back to compensate for the side mid fielder's possible forward shift . Our inside mid fielder's forward shift could be counterbalanced either by a combined movement made by the inside and the center mid fielder (the first moves wide and the second goes to take his place), or with the center mid fielder moving onto the sidelines. In my opinion, however, neither of these two plays are tactically as advantageous as the shift we have shown in the figure. Objectively speaking, it is complicated to get three players to shift together as in the first case, and the second solution would take too long to put into effect.

<u>Focal points.</u>

If we decide to accept the 3 against 3 situation on the back line, the thing we must be most careful about is the defense zone. We will be able to judge the situation on the rest of the field only if we are controlling the opponent's strikers. When and if we see that our defense is able to contain the opposing strikers, we can begin to consider the quality of our mid field pressing, where, in any case, the situation is one of numerical superiority (5 > 4) to our advantage. If our defense section is under too much pressure, we will have to modify the situation, changing strategy, players or system. If we are suffering most in the defense section one solution might be to put in an extra back changing from the original 3-4-2 to a 4-4-2 directed more towards an individual rather than a zonal marking system. The only serious adaptation in such a case would be taking center mid fielder from a position in front of the defense line and placing him behind the three backs to function as a sweeper.

THE 3-5-2 AGAINST THE 3-4-1-2.

We will finish off our survey of how to counteract with the 3-5-2 by having a look at the tactical set up when our team is meeting an opponent using the 3-4-1-2.

<u>The tactical situation.</u>

Looking at the situation superficially, we might suppose that there is numerical equality in the mid field, with our center mid fielder controlling the opposing attacking mid fielder – and in some cases this may be true. Yet the mobility, the technical ability, the class and the sheer charisma of the attacking mid fielder may have a crucial effect on his own range of play, with obvious repercussions on the generic judgement that we have just made. In analyzing the tactical face off between a 3-5-2 and a 3-4-1-2, I prefer to make the following initial considerations. If the opposing N° 10 is more of a in depth mid fielder or an offensive director of play rather than an extra striker, it is, I feel, better to adopt the set up shown in Fig. 75. Sometimes, however, the N° 10 shows clear signs of changing himself into a third striker, moving up vertically and breaking into the goal zone – and in such cases I prefer to begin the match as shown in Fig. 76. In this second line up, we start off with a situation of numerical inferiority in attack (2 < 3), of numerical equality in the mid field (4 against 4) and of numerical superiority in defense (4 > 3). It is clear from this that the center mid fielder is now more an extra back than a real mid fielder. That does not mean, however, that the player in question has to follow the opposing attacking mid fielder wherever he goes on the field as a sort of individual marker. In my opinion

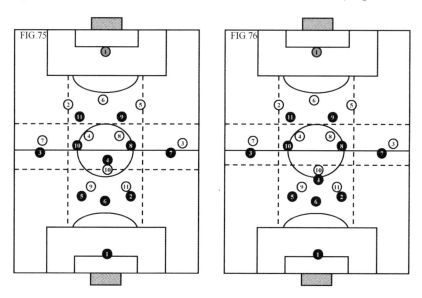

the center mid fielder should go in coverage on the attacking mid fielder when he is playing behind the strikers, leaving the backs to control him when he is moving vertically into depth and acting as an extra striker.

Shifting moves to create numerical superiority.

Having had a good look at the strengths and probable plays of the opposing attacking mid fielder, we can then begin to consider the best countermoves to make in order to contain his range of action and, more generally, to keep a check on the development of the opponent's play. If the attacking mid fielder is acting as an extra striker, we can leave him to the defense section and use the tactical ploys we have already seen when looking at the countermoves to make facing the 3-4-3 (the mid fielders slipping across into the ball zone in order to limit the opponent's space and playing time). If, on the contrary, the rival attacking mid fielder has been asked to move back and to play as the organizer of his team's attack, it will be important to create numerical superiority by having the mid fielders slip into the ball zone – remembering that the opposing center mid fielders generally support play and do not like to accompany attacking moves. Case by case, we will bring our nearest striker back to cover them, so giving our center mid fielder the chance to get near the player in possession. The following figure is an example of what I mean:

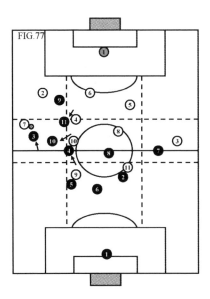

FIG.77

Carrying out offensive pressing implies that our team will have an aggressive conduct of play and means that each section of the team must move into depth, all players being involved in forward shifting. Figure 78, for example, shows the inside mid fielder moving out in pressure on the opposing side back who is in possession. As a consequence of this the center mid fielder moves up to contain the opposing player who is now free.

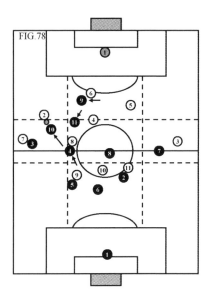

FIG.78

<u>Focal points.</u>

The key to a good match in the defense phase is probably the control of the attacking mid fielder. In the attacking phase, we will have to verify the effectiveness of the duels in mid field (inside and side players). We have already had a look at possible shifts in the defense phase to limit the attacking mid fielder. Should this player be so much above average ability as to put our defense section in continuous danger, then the coach could rectify the situation by modifying the team's system of play. We might decide to sacrifice the center mid fielder, telling him personally to control the opposition's best player and begin playing with a 3-1 (the center mid fielder marking his adversary) -4-2; or we could do without a striker, putting any other player in coverage on the attacking mid fielder (and therefore modifying the system from the initial 3-5-2 into a 3-1-5-1).

Chapter 5

Counteracting with the 3-4-1-2 system

Counteracting with the 3-4-1-2

THE 3-4-1-2 AGAINST THE 4-4-2.

The tactical situation.

Fig. 79 shows the basic counteraction when the 3-4-1-2 is facing an opponent lined up with the 4-4-2. We have a favorable situation in defense (3 > 2). In the mid field the duels will be well-defined (4 against 4), while in attack the attacking mid fielder and our two strikers will be fronted by a four-man defense. Dividing the field into vertical lines, we can see at once that we have a situation of numerical inferiority (1 < 2) on the sidelines. This will be the most important tactical problem to resolve in facing our opponents. To our advantage there is the 3 >2 situation in defense and in attack.

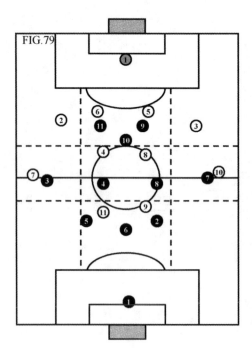

Shifts made to create numerical superiority.

Our defense is playing in numerical superiority against the two opposing strikers and will be able to exploit the fact that the nearby mid fielders can move backwards to double up on the opponents (Fig. 80), but the situation of numerical equality in the mid field will have to be modified to our advantage by the attacking mid fielder's shifting moves.

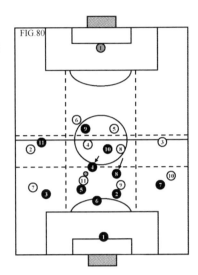

In general, the attacking mid fielder can play in depth (moving up to put pressure on the rival defense players) or come back into the mid field line in order to create a situation of numerical superiority there (5 > 4). The attacking mid fielder's plays are fundamental to ensure that the team is not undergoing a one to one situation along the sidelines. Fig. 81 is an example of a shifting move when the opposing side mid fielder is in possession. Our side mid fielder has gone to put him under pressure, and our nearest center mid fielder is covering a possible pass, while the right center mid fielder shields the defense line and the attacking mid fielder moves back onto the other opposing mid fielder.

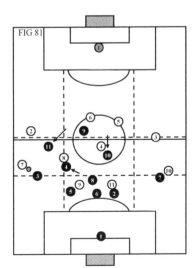

Fig. 82 and 83 show two different shifting moves to be made when the side back is in possession. In the first case, it is our attacking mid fielder who moves sideways to contrast the player in possession, with the mid fielders closing in on the ball zone without losing touch of their direct adversaries. In the second case it is our nearby center mid fielder who comes out to contrast the player in possession, with the attacking mid fielder closing up on the opposing player in support. In this move, my opinion is that the team should be placed further back than in the previous case. In fact our center mid fielder will have to cross a fair distance to get to the ball zone; this will take time, which can be covered correctly only if the phase of transition between attacking and defending is now complete and our players have already managed to re position themselves in a close and compact way.

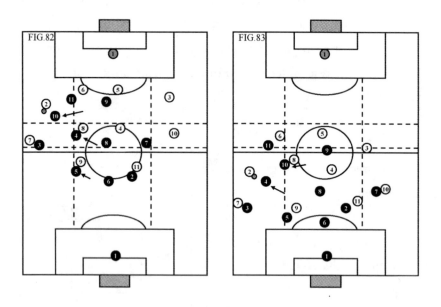

We will end our survey of shifting moves by having a look at the
tactical behavior of the team
when they are involved in in-
depth pressing. The example
shows the striker putting pressure
on the opposing side back in possession, with the team marking in
an aggressive way, shifting forward to close in on players who
may gain possession.

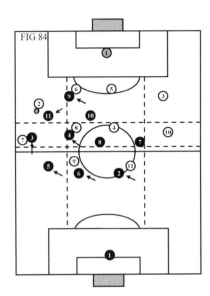

FIG. 84

Focal points.

The coach will have to judge the effectiveness of the shifting moves
carried out to stop the opponents from exploiting the 2 against 1
situation along the sidelines. Another important thing is to keep an
eye on the three-man defense: playing in numerical superiority. They
must show themselves well able to put pressure on their opponents
and close up all their playing space. Should the tactical situation create difficulty for us on the sidelines, we can adopt the following
solutions:

•   Invert the triangle in the mid field. Change from a 3-4-1-2 to
        a 3-5-2. In this way it is easier to slip over to the sidelines
        because we will be shifting forward.
•   Change from a 3-4-1-2 to a 3-4-3, with the side strikers
        ready to act tactically when their team is not in possession.

THE 3-4-1-2 AGAINST THE 3-4-3.

We will now have a look at the situation when we are facing a team using the 4-3-3.

The tactical situation.

Our defense section is in numerical equality (3 against 3) facing a three-man attack playing wide. In the mid field, their center mid fielder will probably be in our attacking mid fielder's zone of play, with their side players facing our inside ones. Our side mid fielders should have playing space along the lines at least until by moving into depth they start to interact with the opposing side backs. Their four strong defense is taking care of our two strikers, but there will probably be many 2 against 2 situations in the center seeing that their side backs will be needed to contain our movements along the sidelines.

Figure 85 is a snapshot of the basic tactical situation.

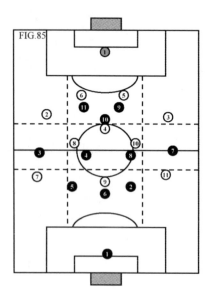

Shifting moves to create numerical superiority.

The most important problem to resolve is how to neutralize the opposing three-man attack. We have already spoken about whether or not it is a good idea to carry out backward shifts to assist the defense section and create a situation of numerical superiority. One thing is sure: if we can bear up to the 3 against 3 in defense, that will help us to play more aggressively; while, should we decide to integrate our defense with another player, we will probably begin to go in pressing at a lower level. In the following figures we give two examples of shifting moves, onto the sidelines on the one hand (Fig. 86) with a team willing to accept the 3 against 3, and, on the other (Fig. 87), a team that cannot run that risk.

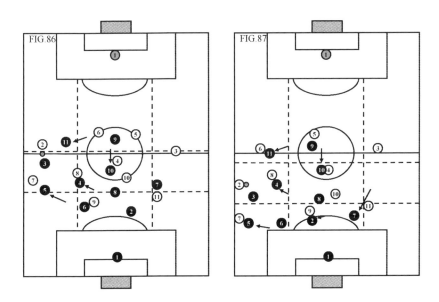

<u>Focal points.</u>

During the match the coach will be following two main things as far as his team's behavior is concerned: just how effectively the three opposing strikers are being counteracted by our defense, and just how good is our timing in moving to put pressure on the opposing side backs when they are in possession. Because of his position at the heart of the system the opposing mid fielder will be the balancing point of our opponent's play and so it is important as well that our attacking mid fielder is managing to limit his range of action. If our shifting moves, or (in cases where we are playing 3 against 3 in defense) if our players are showing signs of insecurity in their duels and thus creating problems for the team, then the coach will have to make the necessary corrections. Let's say we have decided to play in numerical equality against the three opposing strikers and it is this which is creating the difficulty, the coach might decide to adopt a more cautious strategy, bringing one or both the side mid fielders alongside the defense. If the team is not timing their shifts correctly it might be a good idea to reorganize the face-off, choosing a system that is as similar to the opponent's as possible. Taking away a striker and adding a back means that we will start to play with a 4-4-1-1, which is a good system to neutralize the 4-3-3.

THE 3-4-1-2 AGAINST THE 3-5-2.

The main difference between the 3-4-1-2 and the 3-5-2 is the opposite way in which the triangle is lined up at the mid field. With the 3-4-1-2 the attacking mid fielder is at the summit of the triangle, the two center mid fielders interacting at its base. The 3-5-2 does not have an attacking mid fielder but the summit of its mid field triangle is inverted – the single center mid fielder playing further back, and the inside mid fielders more in depth. Let us take a closer look at the lineup.

The tactical situation.

Fig. 88, which highlights the basic lineup of the two teams on the field, is a confirmation of what has just been said.

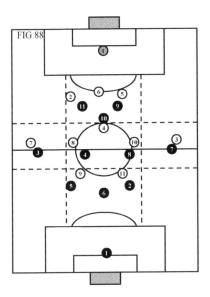

We can see that both systems will have numerical superiority in defense (3 > 2) and equality in the mid field (4+1 against 5). We must keep in mind, however, that the characteristics of the attacking mid fielder can make a big difference to the set up. If our N° 10 is playing near or right behind the strikers the result could be a 3 against 3 in attack and numerical inferiority in the mid field (4 < 5). Our survey of the two teams' vertical lines of play does not high-light anything else, and we can see that there will be well defined duels on the sidelines.

Shifting moves to create numerical superiority.

The basic situation of numerical equality in the mid field will not allow for the systematic application of doubling up in this part of the field. We can create 2 against 1 situations favorable to us, mainly by the backward shifting of the strikers or the attacking mid fielder. The situation of numerical superiority in the defense zone will allow us to take away playing space and go into individual pressure on the opposing strikers. In-depth pressing can be applied by involving the strikers in this sort of play. They will force the opposing defenders' plays, so allowing the mid fielders who are near the ball to become more aggressive. Our mid fielders will also be able to count on the forward shifts made by the backs whenever that may prove necessary. Fig. 89 is an example.

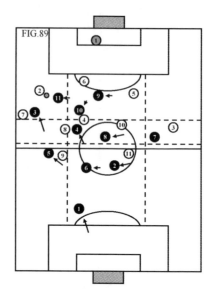

FIG.89

Focal points.

As we have already said, it is not easy to double up in the central part of the field. For this reason, the coach must follow the single duels with attention, and carry out the necessary tactical moves with great care (changing positions or even substituting players). If the situation is becoming serious and our team just cannot put a stop to the opposition's plays, he will even have to consider whether or not

94

to change the system. He might do without the attacking mid fielder
and start playing with a five-man mid field, reflecting the opponent's
set up. In that case, a center mid fielder playing behind the other
mid fielders could give more balance to the situation, helping both
the other players of his section and the defense. Another solution
would even be a 3-5-1-1 situation, bringing on an advanced mid
fielder to substitute a striker. That way we would still be playing with
an attacking mid fielder, who would be useful going in to counteract
the opposing center mid fielder in the defense phase (giving us
numerical superiority in the center of the field), and acting as a connection between the mid field and the only striker to make sure that
he is not completely isolated. Playing with a 3-5-1-1, we will probably have trouble stopping the rival side backs from advancing with
the ball; having to mark a single striker they will now be able to
come forward with greater regularity. Our nearest inside mid fielder
can close in on them, and his place will then be taken by our center
mid fielder who will have to make a forward shift. There is an example of such a move in Fig. 90.

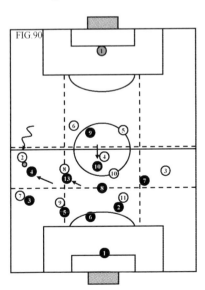

FIG. 90

THE 3-4-1-2 AGAINST THE 3-4-1-2.

The tactical situation.

Fig 91 shows the basic tactical situation we will find when two teams face each other both playing with the 3-4-1-2 system. Both teams will have a situation of numerical equality in defense (2 strikers + the attacking mid fielder against 3 defenders). In mid field the situation is one of equality as well (4 against 4). Looking at the field divided into vertical lines there is no change either: we have numerical equality both on the sidelines and in the center.

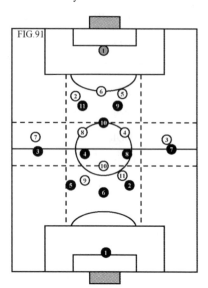

FIG.91

Shifting moves to create numerical superiority.

Controlling the attacking mid fielder will be our biggest problem in the defense phase. As we have already seen in a preceding chapter we can counteract the attacking mid fielder in one of two ways – either by bringing our center defender into depth or by calling a mid fielder back. We can decide which is better only after looking carefully at the strengths and weaknesses of the players (both our own and those of the opposition), at their particular psychological and physical condition and at the specific context of the match itself (the score, the teams' form, environmental considerations, etc.). In any case, Fig. 92 and 93 illustrate both possibilities. We should note that the decision to bring a defender into depth must be associated with in-depth pressing on the part of the team.

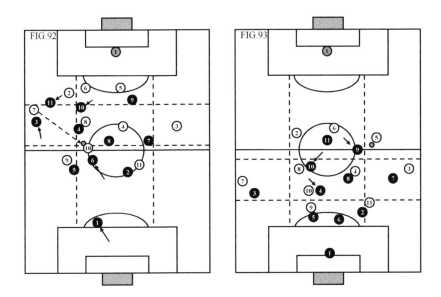

Fig. 93 illustrates the backward movement of the center mid fielder and the simultaneous slipping to the rear on the part of the attacking mid fielder who comes down to cover the zone where a man has been left free.

Focal points.

Having established that both teams' cardinal player is the attacking mid fielder, we must keep a constant eye on how well he is playing and how well he is being controlled. Besides that, the coach will be looking very carefully at the development of the duels in the center of the field and at how the defense is managing to take on the rival strikers. If our forward and backward shifts are taking nothing away from the effectiveness of our opponent's play we will have to think carefully about whether or not to change the system in use. The fundamental thing to consider when trying to face a 3-4-1-2 (without necessarily depending to much on our shifting moves) is the range of action and the overall ability of our attacking mid fielder. If he is the classical offensive attacking mid fielder and does not like to insert himself and play along vertical lines, then the 3-5-2 could be a good solution. Instead, if he is the type of player that just loves going into attack, then it might be a better idea to play with the 5-3-2.

THE 3-4-1-2 AGAINST THE 3-4-3.

The last survey that we will make for the 3-4-1-2 imagines the team facing a 3-4-3 lineup.

The tactical situation.

Both teams are playing with three defenders, four mid fielders and three attacking players. Our offensive pivot, however, is the attacking mid fielder playing behind the strikers, while our opponents have the center of their attack (the center forward) playing in front of the other two strikers at his side. Our survey of the various zones of the field reveals a situation of complete numerical equality. We have 3 against 3 in defense and in attack and a 4 against 4 in the mid field. Even our usual vertical analysis shows that there will be a lot of man to man duels during play. All this can be seen in Fig. 94.

98

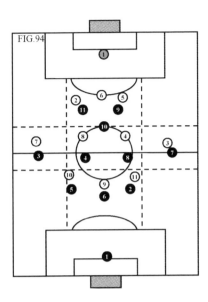

FIG.94

Shifting moves to create numerical superiority.

In order to create a situation of numerical superiority our attacking mid fielder must have good tactical sense and a lot of stamina. His backward moves will be vital if we are to create numerical superiority in mid field. This is all the more important in consideration of the fact that our three backs are locked in with the adversary's three-man attack – and it will be impossible for us to shift forwards with any confidence by means of one of our defense players. Fig. 95 and 96 show how to integrate the attacking mid fielder into the mid field section.

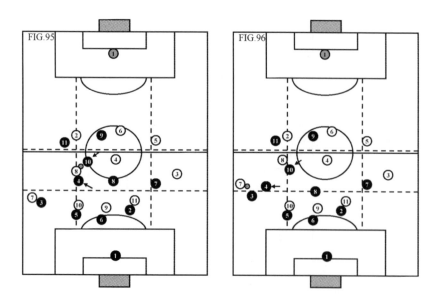

Fig 96 is an example of how the attacking mid fielder moves back on the rival N° 8, who is supporting the player in possession; this move allows the left center back to come out near the ball.

In order to take playing space away from the opposing strikers it is important that the central mid fielders should move back both to shield the defense (blocking off the strikers) and to double up on them. Fig. 97 is an example of what I mean.

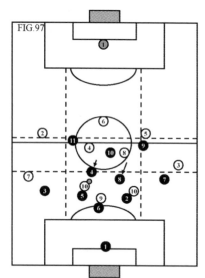

Focal points.

One of the 'hot points' that we must constantly keep our eye on is just how effective our three defenders are in containing the three opposing strikers. Only if our defense section is playing really well should we continue with the three-man defense and make no change in our attitude. Otherwise, if our defense is in trouble and does not seem able to guarantee resistance, we should modify our system without hesitation. Positioning a side mid fielder as a permanent integration of the defense (rather than having him move backwards and forwards as the situation demands) will modify the original set up into a 4-3-1-2, which will probably be more effective in covering the opposition's attacking front. If, having reverted to the 4-3-1-2, we then begin to suffer numerical inferiority in mid field (3 > 4), it may be a good idea to play with a 4-4-2 or a 4-4-1-1. In the first case, the attacking mid fielder will be substituted with a mid fielder and in the second the player going out will be one of the strikers.

Chapter 6

Counteracting with the 3-4-3 system

Counteracting with the 3-4-3.

THE 3-4-3 AGAINST THE 4-4-2.

To conclude our survey we will now turn to the 3-4-3 system, having a look at the tactical situations that come into play when facing various different teams. To begin with, the 3-4-3 facing the 4-4-2.

The tactical situation.

The counteraction between these two teams will be fairly balanced. There is numerical equality in the mid field (4 against 4), while both defense sections are in superiority (4 > 3; 3 > 2) over the rival attacking front. In order to have a clear idea about the situation we must have a close look at how our attack is placed. If our three strikers are playing in compact formation (as in Fig. 98), the opposition will have numerical superiority on the sidelines (their side back and side mid fielder against our side mid fielder), while our team will be able to take advantage of the favorable situation (3 > 2) in the central part of the attacking zone.

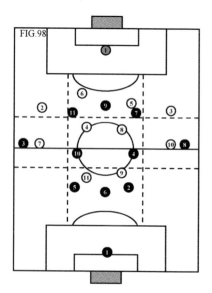

FIG.98

Shifting moves to create numerical superiority.

If we want to create numerical superiority in the mid field we are going to have to use the attacking players – in particular the backward movement of the two side strikers. These can become mobile by getting them to come back to the level of the two opposing center mid fielders or by making them go wide to double up on the sidelines or to absorb the movements of the side backs. Personally, I would opt for the first solution because it does not bring the strikers too far back. Naturally, however, in making any such decision, we would have to keep in mind the strengths and weaknesses of our strikers, not to mention our opponents themselves, and the particular moment of the match. Fig. 99 is an example of doubling up play carried out along the sidelines and made possible by our left side striker moving back and freeing the central mid fielder.

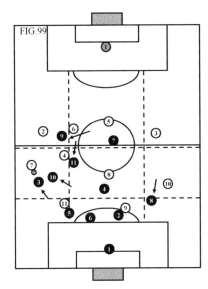

Coming to the defense zone, we are in a situation of 3 > 2. This will enable us to be aggressive in our marking of the strikers, and will allow us to count on the backward doubling up carried out by our mid fielders. Our mid fielders in particular, facing opponents who will not normally go in vertical progression, will be able to move back and double up on the striker in possession when the situation consents this type of play. Fig. 100 is an example.

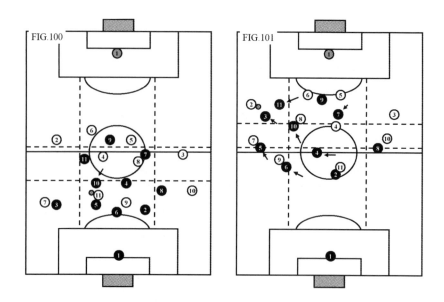

The strikers will have to participate if we want to carry out in-depth pressing – and if possible the side defenders as well, moving up. Fig. 101 is an example, with the side mid fielder moving up towards the opposing side back. At the same time, our side defender is going deep to cover the opponent's side mid fielder, with our striker coming wide to double up on the player in possession.

Focal points.

When facing a 4-4-2 the timing of our shifting moves is the key, making sure that our opponents cannot take advantage of the superiority they have on the sidelines. If we can resolve this all important problem in our favor, then we will probably be able to win the match without too much difficulty. The coach will also have to follow the various duels in the mid field, and, above all, to see that the defenders are able to pull their weight as regards their numerical superiority over the opposing strikers. If our team is not able to contain the rival side mid fielders, it might be a good idea to change our system, correcting the set up on the sidelines where we are having problems. Adopting a 5-4-1 might be a good solution. There are different ways of changing the 3-4-3 into a 5-4-1. We could widen the strikers and put them level with the line of the mid fielders, bringing both the side mid fielders back on a line with the defense section. We could also substitute both side strikers with side backs. Or we could make a change that would include a part of both these moves.

THE 3-4-3 AGAINST THE 4-3-3.

The tactical situation.

Both teams have a three-man attack. Our opponents, however, are facing us with four defenders while our defense line is in numerical equality (3 against 3). This will be compensated for by our numerical superiority in the mid field (4 > 3). The usual 'vertical' analysis shows that we have numerical superiority in the central part of our attack (3 > 2). On the other hand, their three-strong central mid fielders could give us some problems in the center of the field (2 < 3). Our side mid fielders should be relatively free, at least up to the zone covered by their side backs.

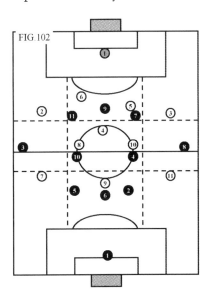

FIG. 102

Shifting moves to create numerical superiority.

Our numerical superiority in the mid field section will enable us to carry out pressing both in depth and in defense. The real difficulty is to take away playing space and time from their mid field's rearguard summit. It is not easy, in my opinion, to bring out one of our mid fielders to put pressure on an opposing player because the resulting situation of numerical inferiority will complicate the situation. The best thing to do is to bring back the nearest member of our three-man attacking front, who will move in to cover the opposing center mid fielder. The whole team will have to work together following the chosen strategy in order to face the 4-3-3 with positive results. In Fig. 103 we can see some examples of shifting moves to be made if you have decided to play an aggressive match, applying in-depth pressing. Our side mid fielder moves up on the opposing side back in

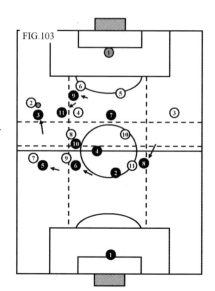

FIG. 103

possession; our left side striker 'blinds' the rival center mid fielder; our center forward closes on the player in support; our center mid fielders put pressure on the opponent's center mid fielders; the side mid fielder on the weak part of the field converges on the defense section and, shortening up on the ball area, the backs move in on their particular strikers. As you can see there are a whole lot of shifting moves to be carried out, and it will be difficult for a team whose maneuvers are nor perfectly synchronized to get so many players to move together with faultless timing.

Defense pressing, on the other hand, comes about through the backward movement of the mid fielders who double up on the striker in possession. A pair formed by a side back + a side mid fielder can double up on the opposing wings, while the center defender + a mid fielder cover the center forward. Fig. 104 and 105 show two examples of rearguard pressing.

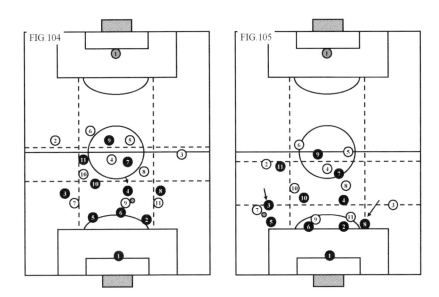

Focal points.

In my opinion the 3-4-3 is not a system that fits in very well with the 4-3-3. Our team must, therefore, be in control of play for a good part of the match if we want to contain the opponents. Apart from this, we will have to keep a careful eye on our defense line's ability to counteract the three opposing strikers, remembering that they will be playing in numerical equality. Only if they are showing a good all round solidity and are winning the majority of their individual duels, should we consider our defense safe and not in need of modification. When we decide to make a change we will have to keep in mind that it is difficult to modify this system without completely deforming our original set up. In my view, the best way of defending against the 4-4-3 is by using the 4-4-1-1, but to arrive to such a system we would have to make a number of radical changes. Choosing a 5-4-1, making all the changes that we have already described, you would have a situation of 5 against 3 in the defense phase, but would not be able to play well in the mid field, where their three mid fielders would be in numerical superiority (3 > 2) in any case. An intermediary solution might be a change to the 4-4-2, even if we would have to make substantial changes to arrive at that (substitution of a striker with a defender, switching from a three to a four man defense and placing one of the strikers more in the middle to convert from a three to a two man attack).

THE 3-4-3 AGAINST THE 3-5-2.

When a 3-4-3 has to face a team using the 3-5-2 you have the problem of limiting numerical inferiority in the mid field – as in the case that we have just been looking at. Let us have a closer look at the situation.

The tactical situation.

Our defense section is in numerical superiority over the two rival strikers (3 > 2). The situation is inverted, however, in the mid field (5 > 4 in the opposition's favor). In attack our compact three-man formation is faced by the same number of defenders in numerical equality. Cutting the field into vertical strips, we see that there will be well defined 'one to one' actions along the sidelines, while in the center the numerical upper hand that we have in defense is confronted by their superiority in the mid field.

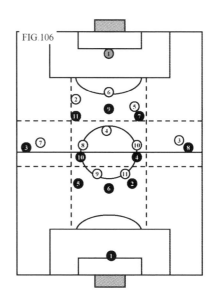

FIG.106

Shifting moves to create numerical superiority.

From what we have already said, we can gather that the most important problem to resolve is connected to the situation of numerical inferiority in the mid field and the space which the opposing center mid fielder will be able to use. If the team is compact and well

organized in its movements we could consider solving the problem by shifting forward through the center. Fig. 107 gives a clear example. At this point, our two defenders will find themselves in numerical equality, and it goes without saying that we can decide to make move like this only if they are not having any difficulty in their individual clashes (especially as far as speed is concerned).

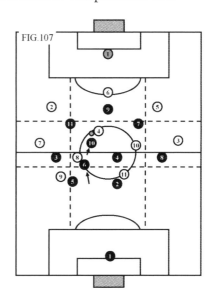

FIG.107

A more convincing alternative (with a 'stand by' defense) would involve bringing a striker back into the area of the opposing mid fielder. This second solution is particularly favorable in my opinion when the opponent is a player who does not very often make incursions in a vertical direction but prefers to move along horizontal lines. In defense our situation of numerical advantage (3 >

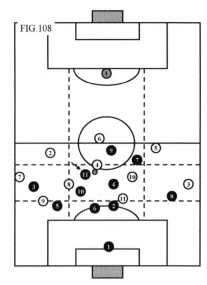

2) can be further improved by having the mid fielder nearest to the opposing striker in possession come back and double up on him.

Wanting to carry out good offensive pressing, the strikers will have to participate, but apart from that the team will have to be capable of shifting into depth. We have already seen in Fig. 107 how to shift forward in the central part of the field. Fig. 109 is an example of a forward shifting move with the ball in possession of the opposing left side back.

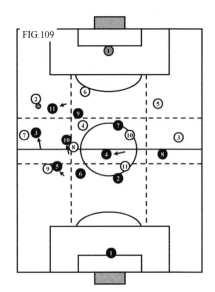

<u>Focal points.</u>

As we have already said, one of the most important problems to resolve derives from the situation of numerical inferiority we are facing in mid field. If the shifting moves that we have suggested are not enough to limit the damage, we could try rectifying the situation by changing the placement of the three strikers. Going from a 3-4-3 to a 3-4-1-2, we line the team up in such a way as to cover the parts of the field where the opposing mid fielders are playing. Apart from keeping an eye on the mid field, the coach will also have to evaluate the situation in the defense zone and the duels on the sidelines.

THE 3-4-3 AGAINST THE 3-4-3.

Our second to last imaginary set up sees both teams using the 3-4-3.

<u>The tactical situation.</u>

In none of the matches we have looked at up to now has there been such a global situation of numerical equality as we get when two teams are placed on the field using the 3-4-3. In defense and attack we have a 3 against 3 situation, while in the mid field the two teams face each other 4 against 4. Our customary vertical line analysis shows the same thing: a situation of equality in every part of the field. We can see this clearly from Fig. 110.

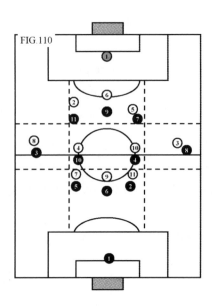

FIG.110

Shifting moves to create numerical superiority.

As the two teams will be playing man to man, the best way to create situations of superiority in the mid field is by getting the side strikers to move back. By sliding down field, these two players can double up on the player in possession, or, by closing in on the player in support, allow the mid fielder to make for the ball zone to get a 2 against 1. Fig. 111 shows left side mid fielder + the left side striker doubling up on the player in possession.

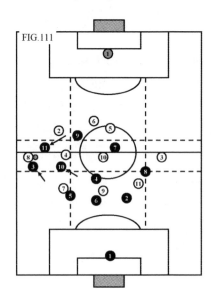

FIG.111

In Fig. 112 on the other hand we can see the right side striker moving back to blind the opponent's supporting center mid fielder. In this way our right center mid fielder can make for the ball and double up on the player in possession.

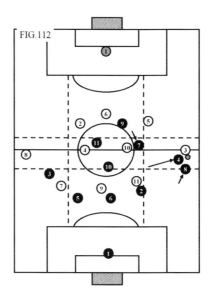

It is easier to create numerical superiority in the defense zone. The following figure gives an example with a center mid fielder moving back to double up on the opposing center forward.

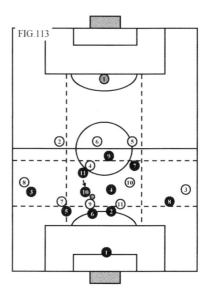

The situation of numerical equality in all parts of the field does not help our forward shifts and as a result we will have to depend on the participation of our strikers to carry out in-depth pressing. Fig. 114 shows a team that is trying to regain possession in the offensive section of the field.

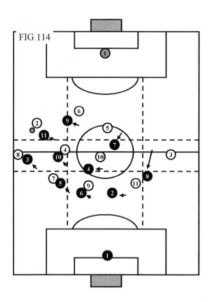

The side striker has come out to put pressure on the player in possession while the center forward makes it difficult for him to dump by closing in on his supporting team mate. In the mid field we are marking the players near the ball as tightly as we can, and the striker on the weak side moves back a yard or two so as to be active if there is a change of front. The side mid fielder furthest from the ball (on the right in the example) goes back as well, so that he can go in combination with the defense line, permitting the backs to close in on the ball zone.

<u>Focal points.</u>

During the match the coach will have to keep an eye on two things in order to judge our team's performance when we are not in possession: the players' one to one duels and the strikers' ability to make themselves tactically useful. Critical situations could depend on the weaknesses of single players or on the structure as a whole. A badly organized team will make the inadequacies of its single players even more evident. In such contexts the coach can intervene by substituting players (perhaps only changing their positions) or by modifying the system. In my opinion, changing the 3-4-3 into a 3-5-2 will help resolve the problems in the mid field. On the other hand if our biggest problem is the control of the opposition's three-man attacking front, we can start to use four men in defense or switch to a 5-3-2 (or even a 5-3-1-1), with the aim of closing up the opposing strikers' playing space.

THE 3-4-3 AGAINST THE 3-4-1-2.

<u>The tactical situation.</u>

In general, the tactical situation here is a reflection of the one we have just been considering above. The opposition's attacking striker, however, may be a player whose range of actions covers a large area of the field, with the result that as the match proceeds his team will at times look like a 3-4-3 and at others more like a 3-5-2. It is very possible then, that from a tactical situation of global numerical equality (as when two teams are both lined up with the 3-4-3) we may suddenly switch to a situation of numerical superiority in defense and inferiority in the center, as when the 3-4-3 meets the 3-5-2.

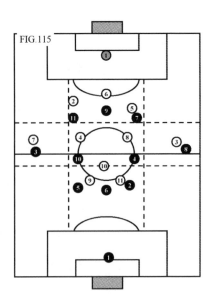

FIG.115

Shifting moves to create numerical superiority.

One of our aims in making the right shifting moves will be to limit the opposing attacking mid fielder's range of actions. As we have already seen, we can reduce the attacking mid fielder's playing time

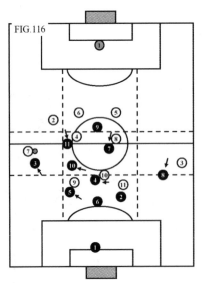

FIG.116

and space by having the three central defenders shift into depth or one of the two central mid fielders move backwards. The 3-4-1-2 system is usually lined up with two offensive mid fielders in support of the attacking mid fielder. In that case, it is probably best for our nearest center mid fielder to mark the opposing attacking mid fielder, leaving the task of covering his supporting players to our side strikers who will move back to do the job (Fig. 116). Making the same type of move, we can double up on the sidelines: our side strikers move back on the players in support, one of our center mid fielders covers the attacking mid fielder, the other closes in on the ball area. As we have already seen in other counter positions of the 3-4-3, it is vital that the mid fielders shift backwards to double up in the defense zone.

Focal points.

The most important thing required of the team is their ability to read and interpret the situation. Their attacking mid fielder gives the opposition great variability, and so we must be ready and alert at all times. When their attacking mid fielder moves back, our team must be able to carry out the objectives that we have already seen when looking at how to counteract the 3-5-2. On the other hand, when the attacking mid fielder is playing near the strikers, our players must adapt themselves to this new situation. If our team does not seem able to react immediately to these continually varying situations, it might be a good idea to modify the playing system. Changing from a 3-4-3 to a 3-5-2 might be a good solution, giving the team tighter points of reference on the field so that they will be depending less on shifting moves.

Chapter 7

Details and preparation

A closer look.

We have made wide use of shifting moves in order to perfect the
way to defend against specific opposition systems. We must always
remember that the ball moves much faster than any player, and that
timing is always vital to correct shifting moves. When we get our
shifting wrong, apart from getting no advantage from what we are
trying to do, we may also be putting ourselves in serious danger. In
order to create perfectly effective shifts, the distances covered by the
players should be short (compact team), the opposing player in possession should not be not free to play the ball with ease (aggressive
team), and our players should not only aware of the collective tactical mechanisms, but able to put them into effect with fluidity. To get
to a point like this, of course, the coach must have prepared the
team both on an individual and a collective level.

Exercises.

In my opinion, psycho-kinetic exercises are what is needed to
improve the individual's (and consequently the team's) ability to
react to the changeable tactical context. As far as collective exercises
are concerned, it is a good idea, coming up to the day of the match,
for the coach show and train the team how to carry out the specific
moves that will help them to contain the opposing system. Here are
some practical suggestions:

1.   specific exercises for the defense section in relation to the
        type of attack set up by the opposition;
2.   specific exercises for the mid field section in relation to the
        type of counter position they are meeting in the opposition's

corresponding section;

3. team exercises for carrying out low level pressing (backward shifts);

4. team exercises for carrying out in-depth pressing (forward shifts).

In the exercises proposed in N° 1 the defense section will be containing the strikers, supported by the mid field. Here the training session will be carried out asking the defenders to make the moves (slipping up or down, shifting, going in to cover) that they will repeat during the match, while the attacking section (positioned as the opponents will be lined up during the coming match) and the mid field are moving the ball around and simulating concrete situations and problems that they will likely encounter.

After this simulated and low intensity session, (in which we will make sure the movements are being executed to perfection), they will then move on the a situation of real play, putting the defense against the attack. We might also introduce a number of 'conditions' so as to force the defenders and the strikers to act and behave in a certain way. Following these developments, the coach will be able to judge his defense section's ability to react at once to real situations rather than the predetermined ones that he was looking at in the moves he was trying out during the earlier session.

The exercises proposed in N° 2 follow the same principles that we have just described, applied this time to training the mid field.

The exercises in N° 3 will help the team take in the movements they must make to carry out low level shifting – slipping to the right or left, horizontal or vertical shifts, recovering position. You can work

11 against 0, simulating the movements to be made; various points of reference can also be placed on the field (cones or flags or other markers) to identify the opposition's system. A further development will be the introduction of one or two opposing sections onto the playing field – followed at last by their whole team. In this way the coach will be in a position to verify the general movement of the team first of all; and then the timing or the team's ability to react in situations of real play.

The exercise in N° 4 is carried out along the lines that we have already explained – only here the team is trying to apply in-depth pressing.

In one last exercise, the team could be carrying out points 1, 2, 3 and 4 with one player missing. That will help the team face up to situations of numerical inferiority if a player has been sent off.

Conclusion.

I have no divine right over the truth, of course; and it was never my intention to write a manual for 'the perfect coach'. All the suggestions I have made in the text are merely my own considerations, though I am sure they will help the reader to create his own ideas, connected above all to the experiences that everyone has come to terms with. Whoever has read anything that I have written before will know how important I consider the exchange of opinions in order to improve and develop our ideas.

I can't give you an exact definition of the word 'science'. I don't believe, however, that it is right to consider soccer a mere game. I don't accept the idea of writing it off as one of those sports in which the facts or the episodes (as the experts love to call them) become so important that they block off any kind of scientific approach or analytical depth. If we look carefully enough at each and every negative episode, we will be able to see errors and responsibilities in connection with the shortcomings of the individual player, the team as a whole or the coach. Only those who are incapable of approaching things in a rational way will end up thinking that soccer is a game, no more; and they will always be forced to save themselves by putting the ball out of play and by repeating clichés to each other. Let me give an example – something that happened to me a month ago after seeing a match in Serie C1 in Italy. The day after the match I get a phone call from a journalist friend of mine, who, not having been able to go to the stadium, asked me what I had thought of the performance of the home team's leading central mid fielder – according to the local press he had played in a banal way, without making in depth passes, trying only to gain possession and initiate countermoves. I told my friend that all that I had heard and read was true, only that I would have changed the adjective 'banal' to 'intelligent' – so reversing the judgement. To sum up, what I said was this:

'Your team was lined up with a 4-4-2, the opponents using a 3-4-3. Being able to count on numerical superiority on the sidelines, the player in question tried only to play in the sense, as, I suppose, the coach had asked him to do. What good would it have been to make long vertical passes when the opposing defense section was in numerical superiority and could put the strikers under pressure as well as covering any space there was in the center?'

I am not, of course, trying to accuse the journalists, who are, in my opinion, absolutely vital, especially when they motivate their verdicts, because they give us a perspective on soccer that is very different from that proposed by the pure technicians. Sometimes it is the technicians who grip onto single episodes, justifying performances in which their team has won the match – attacking all the time let us say, but in a way that I would hesitate to describe as lucid – but have, at the same time, shown themselves as completely unprepared to face the opposition's rare counterattacks. However, beyond the opinions of journalists or coaches, I believe we must all force ourselves not to consider soccer as a mere game. It is true that there is no 'soccer scientist' able to win each and every game, but neither do I know any doctor capable of producing the elixir of eternal life.

Massimo Lucchesi

Other Soccer Coaching Books by Massimo Lucchesi available now from Reedswain Publishing

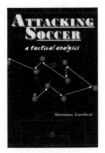

Attacking Soccer
A Tactical Analysis

$14.95

Coaching the 3-4-3

$12.95

Coaching the 3-4-1-2 and 4-2-3-1

$14.95

Soccer Tactics
An Analysis of Attack and Defense

$12.95

For ordering information or to receive a full catalog of coaching books, videos, software and equipment:
Call 800-331-5191

or

visit us on the web at www.reedswain.com